Praise for
Generation Ex

"Anyone who has suffered the experience of their parents' divorce will be blessed by this book. Jen Abbas will gently guide you on the path of personal health and wholeness with her vulnerability, wisdom, and biblical counsel."
—DRS. LES AND LESLIE PARROTT, Seattle Pacific University, authors of *When Bad Things Happen to Good Marriages*

"Jen has written a powerful book with a desperately needed message of hope for a lost generation. What's more, she does it with an honesty that is refreshing and with the intimacy of someone who has walked down this road herself. I was personally moved by the deeply personal revelations in this book, and as a result I have been able to see the issues at work in my family in a much clearer way."
—BRAD MILES, lead vocalist with Everman

"Jen Abbas masterfully weaves practical helps into the vulnerable, honest, and insightful discussions in *Generation Ex*.... Halfway through the pages of this book, I was personally struck again by the overwhelming weight of the emotions of those years surrounding my own parents' divorce, and yet I was struck once more by the hope soaking every page as this revolutionary book wound toward its close. *Generation Ex* will surely free countless broken hearts to sing again."
—FRED STOEKER, coauthor of *Every Man's Battle*

"This is a brilliant book!... Jen Abbas' counsel is as practical as it is profound, and relevant not just for children of divorced couples but for any couple considering a divorce or anyone ministering to the children of divorce."
—GARY THOMAS, author of *Sacred Marriage* and *Sacred Parenting*

"*Generation Ex* is packed with stories gleaned from countless interviews of children of divorce, statistics gathered from a wide range of so████, ███ ████ great interactive ways for readers to work ████ ████ ████ ███ ████ ████ ions resulting from a life thrust upon them ████ ████ ████ ████ ████ ████ ████ ████ par- ents. *Generation Ex* is not a comfortab████ ████ ████ ████ ████ be.

Throughout this book Jen gently yet effectively confronts readers with the hard truth and then gives them the means to begin the healing process."

—TIM WAY, senior buyer with Family Christian Stores

"More research is coming out every day about the long-term effects of divorce on now grown children. As a veteran in the publishing world, Jen Abbas knows where there are holes in the market that need filling. Jen also knows the hurt of growing up in a divorced home and offers practical, biblical help for the millions like her—and like me. *Generation Ex* is a timely resource that meets a major felt need in our country."

—JOHN TRENT, PH.D., president, StrongFamilies.com

"This fine book is an excellent resource for both those seeking healing from the experience of divorced parents and those seeking to minister to them. Jen Abbas weaves together personal stories, practical exercises, and powerful faith in a masterful way that is highly readable and motivating. *Generation Ex* is an essential resource for any professional who wants to understand and guide adult children of divorce through a comprehensive healing process."

—TOM EMIGH, vice president for student development, Cornerstone University

"Jen deals with this very delicate subject of divorce head-on, as only someone with her past family experience can. I have written about divorce in my song 'You're My Little Girl' and am constantly being approached by children of divorced parents who are struggling with the very things talked about in this book. I am so thankful that somebody had the guts to step up to the plate and write a book like this."

—JAMIE STATEMA, member of the vocal group Go Fish

"The lingering effects of divorce will cripple adolescents and attempt to destroy the emotional health of adult children unless hope and healing can be found. *Generation Ex* helps readers take a big step in that healing process, equipping adult children of divorce to own their pain before they disown it and allow the losses in their lives to make them better, more healthy adults."

—GARY SPRAGUE, president, Center for Single-Parent Family Ministry

Generation EX

Generation EX

Adult Children of Divorce
and the Healing of Our Pain

Jen Abbas

With a Forward by
Elizabeth Marquardt

Little Rock, Arkansas

Generation Ex: Adult Children of Divorce and the Healing of Our Pain

© 2004, 2006 by Jen Abbas
All rights reserved
First Edition 2004
Second Edition 2006

11 10 09 08 07 06   1 2 3 4 5 6 7 8 9 10

ISBN-10 1-57229-975-4
ISBN-13 978-1-57229-975-7

Printed in the U.S.A.

Cover Design: Jennifer I. Smith

Details, including names, in some anecdotes and stories have been changed to protect the identities of the persons involved. All excerpts from the journal of the author's parents are quoted with permission.

FAMILYLIFE™

Dennis Rainey, President
5800 Ranch Drive
Little Rock. AR 72223
1-800-FL-TODAY
www.familylife.com

The Abbas Family
Elmer, Chi, Chris, and Jenny
1967–1978

To Dad and Mom:
Thank you for bringing me into this world.
I share your vision to leave it just a little better than I found it.
Thank you for the gift of your journaled history
and your blessing on this project.
I love you both.

Contents

Foreword

Since the late 1960s our nation's divorce rate has skyrocketed, leveling off in the mid-1980s at its current rate of almost one in two first marriages. In the early days of widespread divorce, experts assured divorcing parents that, so long as they were happy, their children would be happy too. A generation of studies and the stories of many young people have shown that reality is not nearly as reassuring. In fact, numerous studies confirm that children of divorce are two to three times more likely to suffer serious, long-term social and emotional problems.

For years, research and social debate stalled with the question of how "damaged" the children of divorce are. Yet most grown children of divorce will tell you that they do not see themselves as "damaged goods"— but neither, they will say, was the divorce and their childhood itself "fine." These young people are deeply shaped by their parents' divorce even if they become relatively successful—or very successful—later in life.

A new generation (my own) is leading the divorce debate now, and many of us ourselves grew up in divorced families. We want to know how many children are seriously damaged by divorce, but we have countless other questions too: How does childhood divorce shape the relationships that young people have with their future partners and spouses? With their aging parents? With their own children? How does divorce shape the inner lives of young people? Their moral development? Their spiritual journeys? Their religious identities?

In Jen Abbas's book, readers will find all these questions explored, and more. Abbas is an astute observer of the heart—her own and those of the many young people she talked with. She has turned the pain of her family-of-origin experience into a gift to others who are seeking answers, healing, and wholeness. Readers who grew up in divorced families will find achingly familiar insights in this book. Abbas writes: "For years, our successes at school and work have been heralded as examples of our resilience, when in reality, it was our dogged pursuit of perfection and our insecurities about our own worthiness that fueled the fires of our ambitions." She says that we children of divorce share extraordinary losses: the loss of "stability," "financial security," "continuity," "shared history," "deep intimacy with both parents," as well as "loss of innocent trust when it comes to love and marriage." We even lost "the freedom to express this sense of loss," because the culture wanted so badly to believe that divorce, simply by becoming common, was not so bad for children after all. This message made the pain even worse. As Abbas writes, "Negating our devastation is as destructive as ignoring it," and I would say that denying pain is one of the worst things we can do to a child. Yet this is not a depressing book.

Jen Abbas supports readers as she leads them to confront their past and, once healed from it, face their future with confidence in their new life. She shows readers that there is a new identity possible for them, not as children of divorce but as children of God. Those who have emerged from fragmented, broken families—full of losses and confusing twists and turns—can enter into a new story, journeying with the body of Christ toward the place of peace and wholeness that God wants for us all. The task of the church is to turn away from the divorce-embracing messages of the culture and to recognize the manifold losses felt by the children of divorce and by divorced parents too. Only by recognizing the real losses can the church truly embrace all those affected by divorce and make a place of welcome for these children, young people, and families who so desperately need a spiritual home.

ELIZABETH MARQUARDT is the author of *Between Two Worlds: The Inner Lives of Children of Divorce* (Crown, 2005) which reports a national study of the moral and spiritual lives of grown children of divorce.

Acknowledgments

To My *Abba Daddy:* Thank You for adopting me and giving me Your name.

To My Prayer Team: I simply could not have done this without your encouragement and prayer. Thank you!

To the Steps and Halves That Make Me Whole: John and Pat, Carole, Chris and Kelly (I'm so proud of you!), John and Mary, Jake and Meagan, Carisa and Andy, and Liz.

To My Cloud of Witnesses: Ang, Jen, Melissa, and Rach. Thank you for being my family of friends, my cheering section, my safe place. I love you!

To the Meyers, Schindlers, Willemsens, and Wards: Thank you for filling my emotional scrapbook with pictures of family.

To My Adopted Family, the Kennedys: Dan, Sara, Zach, Noah, Mia and Hannah. Thank you for sharing your GR life with me. I love you more than I knew I could.

To the Community at KCC: Thank you for your prayers, support, encouragement, and inspiration.

To My Friends: I am blessed beyond measure to know you. Though I can't name each of you here, your fingerprints are all over these pages.

To the GR Guild: Shelly Beach, Ann Byle, Lorilee Craker, and Tracy Groot. You guys never cease to amaze and inspire me! Cynthia Beach, Angela Blycker, Sharon Carrns, Katrina DeMan and Alison Hodgson ... welcome to the craziness that is our group!

To My Author Friends: John Trent, Michelle McKinney Hammond, Sherrie Eldridge, and especially Fred Stoeker and Gary Thomas. Thank you for believing in me and confirming this calling.

To My Brain Team: Much love and appreciation to the team that helped me after I knocked my noggin': Dr. Vandenberg, Dr. Fuller, Dr. Opolka,

Molly, Kerri, Grant, and Jen. Thanks for helping me make peace with the new me.

To Three Men: To those who taught me that love is more than theory: the one I loved, the one who loved me, and the one I long to meet, thank you for leaving your marks on my heart.

To Judith Wallerstein: Thank you for giving a voice to those who were unable to articulate their pain. Millions of us can begin to heal because you were brave enough to acknowledge and affirm our hurts.

To Elizabeth Marquardt: It's an honor to share this platform with you.

To My First Publishing Team: Your work turned my musings into something amazing. Thank you!

To My FamilyLife Publishing Team: Amy, Ben, Bob, Dennis, Gregg, Jenni, Keith, Tim, and others behind the scenes. I'm thrilled to partner in the important work you do. Thank you for giving this book new life.

To My Webmaster: Kevin McNeese (www.kmwebdesigns.com) How could I forget you? Thanks for letting me be your guinea pig.

To Those Who Shared Their Stories: Thank you for your honesty. May this book bring you the same peace I have found.

To My Reviewers: Dr. Cherie Winters, Damon, Janice, Jenni, Patti, Rach, and Steph. Your insights made my manuscript better. Thank you.

To the Musicians Who Created the Soundtrack for This Book: Thank you for using your talent to sing what I couldn't say. (Visit my website and blog to see the ever-growing songlist.)

To My Readers: It was the hope of your healing that kept me going when the task seemed daunting. My most fervent prayer is that our generation will realize our utter need for God—in our lives, in our goals, and in our marriages. Let's not bring another generation into this world to experience what we have survived. Let us be the ones to break the cycle of divorce and usher in a legacy of healthy marriage. This book was written for you.

Generation EX

the eruption

divorce
is like a trembling earthquake
the world shakes
rumbling with rage
and all the anger
guilt
and frustrations
that have been festering for so long
below the surface
suddenly spew upward
in an inferno of hate
or apathy...
at times
the earth calms
and you think
the turmoil is over
settled
stable
but
then the cycle begins again
repeating
repeating
repeating
you are weary
you want to rest

and that is when you realize
the shaking has stopped
but
there is an eerie feeling
lurking in the air
you are hesitant to believe
anything
anymore
you are so tired
after struggling for so long
and so you rest
on the one last solid patch of land
only to watch it split in two
two
separate
distinct
parts
that will never
come together
again
each new patch
supports part of you
and as you watch
they pull away.

—JEN ABBAS, AGE EIGHTEEN

Let the Healing Begin

I f you had asked me when I was in high school to describe myself, I would have given you a detached litany of events: Mom and Dad divorced when I was six. Mom married John when I was seven. Dad married Carole when I was fourteen. If you had asked me again when I was in college, I would have added that Mom and John divorced when I was eighteen and John remarried when I was nineteen. I would have described this branching of my family tree nonchalantly, priding myself on my admirable ability to adapt and accept.

As I entered adulthood anticipating my hard-earned independence, I was stunned to discover that my parents' divorces seemed to affect me *more* each year, not less. Even though I was successful academically and professionally, I found myself becoming more insecure each year about my emotional abilities. As I began to see my friends marry, I started to question my ability to successfully create and maintain intimate relationships, especially my own future marriage. I began to see how the marriages—and divorces—of my parents had influenced my relationships, especially when it came to trust. And when it came to love, I was paralyzed because what I wanted so desperately was that which I feared the most.

These thoughts sent me scurrying to scour the shelves of my favorite bookstore. I was looking for answers. But more than anything else, I wanted to know I was not destined to live up to the dismal expectations society had lowered for me. Over and over again, I left the store empty-handed. What I found in the sparse divorce section were books directed toward couples in the process of divorce, books explaining divorce to small children, thick sociological studies, and clinical recovery books. I didn't want to read the pessimistic opinions of a detached scientist. I needed to find hope! I wanted to find healing! I needed to learn how to be vulnerable, trusting, and committed in my friendships. More than anything, I desperately wanted to believe I was not destined for divorce. Since the books I found for children of divorce were almost exclusively about *them*, I felt compelled to write one about *us*, adult children of divorce.

Maybe you're reading this and thinking, *I don't know. My parents are divorced, but we seem to have come out okay. Why look back? The past is past, and I am who I am.* Perhaps your parents worked hard to have an amicable parting. Perhaps they were both supportive and involved in your life, and maybe you were even able to see the positive: "I had a place in *two* great families."

Even if you think you don't have any lingering issues, I invite you to discover how the divorce has shaped your life. You did not experience the fullness of what God designed for you in a family, and so you *have* been hurt. It's just that you are part of a generation that has learned to see these scars as normal.

Think about it. If you glue two pieces of wood together and then pull them apart, it is impossible to make a clean break. As children, we were the glue that bonded our parents together. When they divorced, they may have thought they made a clean break, but we are the splintered remains of their parting. Regardless of *why* our parents divorced, the fact remains that their divorce hurt us. The purpose of this book is not to revisit whether our parents should have worked things out. That's their issue. The purpose of this book is to give us permission to admit it hurt *and* to instill us with hope that we can choose to begin to heal that hurt.

The next few chapters might be a bit hard to read. The tone may strike you as a little dark, but our look back is a necessary step. Though it's painful, acknowledging where we've been in the context of who we are allows us to develop a framework for the hope and healing we desire. So bear with me, because things are going to get a whole lot better as we work through this book.

The issues of divorce are extremely volatile. Some parents are still so sensitive and guilt-ridden that the mere intimation of the possibility that their children may have lingering hurts puts them in a defensive mode. Some children of divorce want so desperately to deny any damage from their parents' divorce that the slightest cast to the past raises walls strong enough to fortify Fort Knox. Society tells us to deal with our loss and try not to make our parents feel guilty, because they have their own issues to deal with. While we do need to extend grace and acknowledge that our parents did not intentionally hurt us, we cannot heal until we first affirm and grieve our pain.

I have a confession for you. When it comes to the impact of divorce on my life, I haven't come to a point of complete closure. And you may not have either...and that's *okay!* Through the years we will experience countless trigger events that will cause us to face the implications of our parents' divorce again and again. I don't say this to discourage you, but rather to encourage you to have realistic expectations. We may not always understand why certain things happen to us, but we can choose to seek the good in them.

You need to know that this book is written from a Christian perspective. If you don't share my faith, you're still going to find a lot of hope and help in this book. However, the things I'm going to ask you to do will likely be more difficult for you. The road to healing requires a willingness to forgive, to make peace, to see the best, to trust, to be whole. These attitudes are not easy to cultivate without divine help.

Frankly, I think it's impossible to forgive others until we understand our own innate need for forgiveness, to love unconditionally until we fully receive Love that has no conditions, and to experience peace that defies human understanding when we seek that peace from circumstances beyond our control. I wonder if you'll come to a point, as I did, when you are so frustrated with your inability to control your circumstances that you'll finally run, exhausted and overwhelmed, to the God who willingly took your hurts and sins upon Himself on the cross, who loves you unconditionally, and who provides a peace you can't explain.

THE BACK STORY

The book you now hold in your hands has its roots in a journal passed between my parents from the early days of their courtship until the day their divorce was final. Although my mom penned the first entry, it was Dad who completed it as he sought an outlet to process the breakup of his marriage and the life-altering ramifications of a newfound faith in God.

My stepmom gave me the 122-page treasure when I was in college. At the time, I was still reeling from the second divorce; I couldn't possibly revisit the first. So I packed the journal away with the rest of my collection of "old life" memories and forgot about it. I'm a thinker, not a feeler, and I've often attempted to deal with my emotional issues by ignoring them or running away from them. I filed that box of journal pages away and moved far from my family. Out of sight and out of mind…or so I thought.

Four years later I told my pastor about my desire to move past the fears that paralyzed me. I realized I had holes in my history, and as I looked ahead, I feared I was missing the pieces I needed to form the foundation of my future. I had so many unanswered questions: I wanted to know that my parents once loved each other. I wanted to know why. I wanted to know how things fell apart, and I especially wanted to know what I could do to avoid following in their footsteps. In talking with my pastor, I remembered the gift I had stashed away. The journal that God prompted my parents to prepare for me—five years before my birth—had waited for this day to be revealed.

Within that text, Dad and Mom were able to tell me, in their own words, not only *that* they loved each other once, but also *why.* They shared memories from their courtship, their wedding, my brother's birth, and my own birthday. I was able to hear them tell me what they had hoped for their life together. I read firsthand accounts of their love, of their loss, of their fears and their failures. I also discovered two imperfect people who fell victim to the world's theory that the goal of marriage is to make us happy, not holy. Like so many other couples my parents' age, they learned the hard way that desire alone cannot hold love together.

It was my dad's hope that the feelings and insights captured in their journal would benefit those who came after him, most especially my brother and me. I began to type up the contents of the handwritten journal so I could easily access the sense of family history I had finally discovered. As I typed, I saw the pieces of my life fit together for the first time in one fluid stroke. Before reading the journal, the timeline of my life had been divided into three distinct segments:

- my life with Dad and Mom—of which I had no recollection—until I was almost seven
- my life with Mom and my stepdad, John (who were married from the time I was seven till I was eighteen)
- the life that began when I became a Christian at age nineteen

The journal provided a means of connecting the segments. I began making notes, adding my own memories of particular events, as well as insights I sensed God whisper to me as I typed. My parents' journal became my workbook toward healing as God filled my mind with His truth. The most important lesson He imparted to me was that I am no longer a victim of my parents' past. I am His precious child with a future full of promise—and so are you!

DIVORCE IS NOT OUR DESTINY

Instead of choosing to focus on what we, as adult children of divorce, missed, we have the incredible opportunity to embrace what we, as Christians, have gained. It is in our relationship with Christ—not in our disjointed families, not in our human relationships, not in our own marriages—that we find our completeness. I believe that God's desire for believers—of all backgrounds—is to strive to be His image-bearers, to derive our identities from our relationship to Him. When we do this, we can overcome the unhealthy tendencies we may have inherited from our families and prepare ourselves for marriage to another imperfect human. We'll also be able to prepare ourselves to be the bride of Christ and to demonstrate His inexplicable, wonderful love to others. As Christians, we are called to a different standard of relating to others, but our experiences as children of divorce may present unique obstacles to living up to those standards. This book is written for those who struggle to reconcile the grace of their heavenly Father with the faults of their earthly parents. We are not destined to follow our parents' tradition of divorce. As Christians, we love God, bear the name of His Son, and are empowered by the love we receive from Him to love others until the day He calls us home.

THE JOB AHEAD

This is a book about letting go: letting go of ill will, self-pity, crushed expectations, broken dreams, lost ideals, and false identities. You have survived the divorce or divorces of your parents. You have discovered—or at least are open to discovering—a faith in a loving God who heals. Maybe you're married, and you're struggling because the ideal marriage you assumed you'd have is not measuring up to your expectations and you don't know how to make it better. This book is for you. Maybe you want to get married, but you're scared. What confidence can you have in building a healthy, joyful marriage when you didn't have the opportunity to see committed love demonstrated at home? This book is for you. It's time to let go. Your parents did the best they could. They never married with the intention to divorce. They're human, and they failed. Let go. Let go of your fear. Let go of your discouragement. Let go of your frustration. Let go of your bitterness. Let go of your pain. *Let go.*

How to Get the Most Out of This Book

Make no mistake: This is not beach reading. This is heart healing. This book will require a lot of reflection and dedication as you work through issues you may not have realized were affecting you. Your attention may be drawn to different points with each subsequent reading because healing comes in layers. What you may not have been ready to see at first may scream out at you later. As you embark on the hard road ahead, consider the following suggestions to guide your way:

- *Be Open.* Just picking up this book is a big step! Believe that you can change who you are despite the template your parents modeled for you. Throughout this book, I use the analogy of snapshots as a way of developing the new template we want to create. As we visualize a clear picture of our desired goals, we can be intentional about creating that reality.

- *Take Your Time.* Take time to reflect, to record your thoughts and feelings, to decide how to make this book an intensely personal guide for improving your life and relationships. Read a chapter, then take some time to let the concepts sink in. Digest it carefully and prayerfully. Healing takes time.

- *Use a Journal.* Each chapter includes questions for reflection. Most likely, memories and feelings will be released as you read; the questions are designed to help you process them. Write your responses to what you read. Underline and write down passages that resonate with you and explain why they do. Make a list of unfinished business you need to address. Healing flows through our pens and word processors. Think of your journal as a way of capturing your feelings so they land in a secure place.

- *Find a Safe Group.* Find a few others who share your experience and invite them to work through this book with you. You will find comfort in knowing you are not alone in your struggles.
- *Give Yourself Permission to Mourn.* All this reflection may take a toll on your emotions. You may feel listless or exhausted. Or maybe you'll become crankier. Your tear ducts may go into overdrive. Perhaps you haven't allowed yourself to cry for years. The scene from *The Prince of Tides* comes to mind. In one emotional moment, Tom Wingo questions, "Why cry? It won't bring him back." Dr. Lowenstein's reply applies to us as well, "No, but it might bring you back."

  Your body compensates for the stress you are facing in examining your past. So take extra care of yourself. Surround yourself with supportive friends. Eat well. Get plenty of exercise. And sometimes the most refreshing thing you can do is take a long nap!
- *Invite God to Be Part of the Process.* Each of us needs to discover for ourselves what we believe. Our personal Christian faith provides context for our suffering, is a source for our hope, and offers healing for our hurts. Invite God to walk with you through the painful parts as He brings you to the healing and wholeness you seek. Each chapter begins with statements of effect and hope. The effect statement acknowledges our hurt; the hope statement affirms our healing.
- *Change Your Thinking.* It's easy to say we won't repeat our parents' mistakes, but unless we intentionally fill our minds and lives with

truth and develop habits of faithfulness, commitment, and unconditional love, we set ourselves up for failure. Each chapter has
a key biblical verse that reinforces the principle presented. Write
down that verse and memorize it as you replace the lies you may
have internalized with truth that will heal you.

- *Share.* I hope this book will help you articulate some of the
  struggles you've had. After working through it, give copies to
  your siblings, parents, and significant others. Not only will it give
  them insight into your life but it may also provide a bridge for
  conversations too long unspoken.

- *Don't Expect to Finish.* This might sound odd, but we may never
  experience once-and-for-all closure. Our parents' divorce will
  always affect us—but we can still achieve continual closure. The
  key is to grieve our losses and hurts as we become aware of them,
  then respond to them in a way that more closely reflects healthy
  character than our learned reaction. Each chapter ends with a
  challenge. If the challenges seem overwhelming or impossible the
  first time through, consider them goals to work toward.

Throughout this book, I'll relate parts of my story, as well as stories of
other adult children of divorce who have shared their lives with me. The
divorce experience is vast and varied, so I collected extensive surveys from
over sixty other children of divorce, conducted in-depth interviews with
another dozen, and engaged in countless informal chats with children of
divorce through e-mail, my Web site, and casual conversations. I'm confident you'll find your experience reflected somewhere within these pages.
To provide balance and perspective, I also talked at length with six happily married couples who each shared wonderful bits of wisdom from
their thirty-plus years of marriage.

I'm not a counselor. I'm not a pastor. But I'm not an outsider to this
topic. It's personal to me because I have wrestled with the ramifications of
divorce and sought hope for my own healing. I admit I don't have all the

answers, but I do have hope. I do have peace. I do have joy. Growth is a process, and I want to share with you how to discover the hope I have found.

Would you join me in choosing to create a different legacy for our lives?

Our Story

Since 1970 divorce has affected over a million children each year. According to recent statistics, more than half of all children will experience the divorce of their parents by their eighteenth birthday.[1] Of these, over half will also see the breakup of a parent's second marriage. Another 10 percent will go on to witness three or more family breakups, all before age eighteen.[2] These numbers don't even take into account those who face their parents' divorce as adults. Today, more than 40 percent of all American adults between ages eighteen and forty are children of divorce.[3]

But these statements represent more than sad statistics to us. Those of us who grew up in the '70s and '80s are the first divorce generation, Generation Ex. Despite the assuring claims of *Cosmo* and company—which convinced our parents that our well-being depended more on their happiness than their commitment—society is now beginning to realize what we have known all along: Divorce is not simply a bump in the road for the children affected by it.

Can you identify?

- You're afraid of falling in love but really want to.
- You've turned into a perfectionist.
- You're afraid that even though someone says, "I love you," ultimately that person might leave you.
- For you, trust comes in hard-earned degrees.
- You're not sure where home is, or you aren't so sure you want to accept the home that society has defined for you.

- You wonder if you will ever have your entire family in the same room without fighting or awkward silence.
- You have holes in your history.
- You aren't sure what a healthy marriage looks like.

All these are typical effects of divorce on children. Divorce alters our identities. It clouds the lens through which we understand the world. It weakens the foundation of our emotional development. As children, we likely were not able to comprehend the difference between our parents not loving each other and not loving us: Why would a daddy who says he loves me choose not to live with me? If Mommy is the center of my world, why am I not the center of hers?

Many of us stuffed our feelings of betrayal, rejection, fear, anger, and abandonment. In the backs of our minds, we consoled ourselves with the hope that things would get better when we were on our own. However, after we left the nest, our parents' divorce continued to affect us. As we seek our own romantic relationships, we discover we don't know how to create what we desire, and the fear that we'll re-create what we've left behind consumes us.

If our parents' decision to divorce were truly a healthy one because it offered the potential for a happier home, then why do so many of us still struggle decades later with issues of abandonment, trust, commitment, and making our own marriages work?

Divorce is often *the* defining event of our life, and the implications of our parents' choice continue to ripple throughout our life.

SOCIAL HISTORY

This news makes a lot of people squirm. As children of divorce, we certainly don't want to believe that our hurts will last a lifetime. We'd much rather believe the lie we've been told: that the divorce—and its impact on us—is in the past.

We live in a country where people value independence and will fight to defend their entitlements. The fundamental right to divorce has become as cherished an American tradition as baseball and apple pie.

When Governor Ronald Reagan of California signed the first no-fault divorce law into effect in 1969, the cultural gatekeepers heralded the event as a major victory for the betterment of marriage. The thinking was that if couples were free to—without assigning blame—end marriages that did not fulfill them personally, then the marriages they would subsequently enter would be more satisfying. This marked a significant shift in the universal understanding of the purpose of marriage. As Barbara Dafoe Whitehead explains in her book *The Divorce Culture*, prior to the late '60s, marriage was seen as a societal obligation. Society at large placed great pressure on couples to work out their differences so they could raise healthy, well-adjusted children who would become productive members of society. After the late '60s, marriage was seen as a choice of personal expression. With that choice came the freedom, even the right, to choose to leave the marriage if it was no longer bringing about the personal satisfaction a man or woman expected.[4] Popular literature assured our parents that divorce was like any other crisis and, after a short period of transition, we would all recover, if not be better for it. Happier parents made for better parents and, in a sort of trickle-down philosophy, happier children. As a result of this shift in law and attitudes, the number of "expressive divorces" climbed steadily. Statistics have shown that despite the former partners' hope that they could find more happiness in a second marriage, second attempts are more likely to end in divorce (60 percent) than first marriages (50 percent).[5]

A LONE VOICE IN THE SOCIOLOGICAL WILDERNESS

This paradigm shift in thinking intrigued Dr. Judith Wallerstein, widely considered the world's foremost authority on the long-term effects of divorce. In 1971, she began a longitudinal study of sixty divorced parents and their 131 children. The study included in-depth interviews with parents and children for a six-week period following the final separation and again at eighteen months, five years, ten years, fifteen years, and twenty-five years following the divorce. The results, which she details in her books *Second Chances: Men, Women and Children a Decade After Divorce* and *The Unexpected Legacy of Divorce,* are sobering. At the fifteen-year mark, these children, now in their late twenties and early thirties, were struggling to establish secure love relationships of their own. Each day they were still reliving the feelings of betrayal, abandonment, and rejection. Fifteen years after the crisis, the divorce still formed the template to which each relationship was compared. Many of those children who seemed to adjust well to their parents' divorce as children experienced as adults what Wallerstein calls the "sleeper effect."[6] At each crucial passage of the child's life—and most especially when the child attempted to form his or her own romantic relationships—the impact of the divorce struck with renewed intensity, crippling the adult child's ability to create healthy attachments. (We'll discuss the sleeper effect more thoroughly in chapter 8.)

Wallerstein's book was not received well because it ran counter to what society wanted to believe. It was, however, embraced by Christians and family-rights organizations, a great irony in that Judith Wallerstein does not profess to be a Christian and isn't an advocate of marriage at all costs. Admittedly, her sampling was a small representation of white, middle-class Americans in a single California county. But her purpose was simply to chronicle the experience of divorce by measuring the emotional effects. As I read her book, I found myself thinking, *This is me!* Reading Wallerstein's book assured me that I'm not the only adult child of divorce who struggles to reconcile past, present, and future.

But despite Wallerstein's research, the controversy surrounding divorce continues.

AN EXAGGERATION?

In January 2002, E. Mavis Hetherington and John Kelly caused quite a stir with their book *For Better or for Worse: Divorce Reconsidered.* The authors asserted that research shows that lifelong effects of divorce are greatly exaggerated. While they concede that divorce does have negative effects, the researchers found that only 20 to 25 percent of children of divorce suffered long-term damage—defined as lasting social, emotional, or psychological problems—as opposed to just 10 percent of adults from intact families.[7]

Elizabeth Marquardt, an affiliate scholar with the Institute of American Values and a child of divorce, took issue with this conclusion in a 2002 *Washington Post* article. She wrote:

> I've interviewed dozens of young adults from divorced families. The details vary, but all tell stories equally complex.... Because I met with college graduates, most of the people I was interviewing had achieved a certain level of success. If you gave them a questionnaire and asked, for instance, if they had ever been arrested, dropped out of school or been diagnosed with a mental illness, practically every one of them could respond "no." But that does not mean they were unaffected by their parents' divorce.
>
> Those of us who have experienced the losses of divorce know the truth. I'm 31 years old. I'm a writer, just as I always wanted to be. I have a graduate degree from the University of Chicago, a loving husband and supportive family and friends. From the outside, I look pretty successful. But I have a complex story that, especially through my early years, was largely shaped by my parents' divorce....
> I have never doubted their love for me. But for as long as I can remember, they led completely separate lives. I lived with my mother during the school year and my father during summers and

holidays. I did not lose either of my parents, but a reunion with one was always a parting from the other, and the longing I felt for each of them produced sadness and a fear of loss that persisted when I grew up. Their divorce doesn't explain all that I am, but the way it shaped my childhood is central to understanding who I am.[8]

For adult children of divorce, our parents' divorce is the Achilles heel to our well-being. For years, our successes at school and work have been heralded as examples of our resilience, when in reality, it was our dogged pursuit of perfection and our insecurities about our own worthiness that fueled the fires of our ambitions. Our "well-adjusted acceptance" was more a desperate effort to restore peace and stability to our fluctuating families. Our activities simply offered an escape from the stresses at home. As the tensions increased—before and after divorce papers were signed—so did our proficiencies. Football drills were nothing compared to enduring the sparring between Mom and Dad. The collective cacophony of squeaky violins, pulsing drums, pounding keyboards, and amplified guitars not only required our concentration but also provided more consolation than the sounds of silence.

WE PAY THE PRICE

In her book, Wallerstein focuses on the effects of divorce on parents as well as children, and while her research finds that divorce has mixed results for the parent, it shows that overwhelmingly, divorce is a losing situation for children. Her key reason for this conclusion? Divorce is the only crisis where parents put their own wants before children's needs. In defense of the divorcing couple, the decision to divorce is often thought of as a means to providing a better environment for their children, because ideally, the breakup of the marriage will pave the way for a happier home.

In reality, however, parents establishing separate households often tend first to their own needs. As Wallerstein so aptly wrote, "In the crisis of divorce, mothers and fathers put children on hold, attending to adult problems first."[9] If our custodial parent pursues a new love relationship during this transition, our feeling of being second priority deepens. We miss out on the nurturing we need when our parents are licking their wounds or looking outside the home for a comforting salve. We need parents, and the best we sometimes get is a roommate. While a parent understands that this upheaval comes with the transition, the child whose emotional growth is stunted does not know the chaos is temporary.[10]

Our perspective on the divorce differs vastly from that of our parents. We do not perceive divorce as a second chance, and this is part of our pain. Divorce shatters our sense of home. As much as our parents strive to convince us otherwise, we still feel rejected because the thing we expect as our right—stability for our formative years—has been taken away without our approval.

Custody arrangements are often made for our parents' convenience, not our growing needs. As teenagers, we are forced to choose between spending time with friends or our other parent. What should be the natural process of establishing independence becomes an agonizing source of guilt. If we choose the football game and homecoming dance over a weekend with Dad, what does that tell him about our feelings toward him? Divorce is a price *we* pay as our parents fail to fulfill our unspoken expectation: Parents are supposed to make sacrifices for us, not vice versa.[11]

Finally, after years of being the objects of intellectual discussion, we have reached an age where we can speak for ourselves.

GENERATION EX SPEAKS

In his October 4, 2002, article in the *Washington Times,* Steve Beard examined the plethora of divorce-inspired songs in light of the commercial success of Pink's "Family Portrait." He wrote, "Pink's lyrics touch a raw nerve in a generation that grew up with ringside seats to divorce and abandonment. While their parents were singing songs of protest about foreign wars and civil rights, a new breed of songwriters relates more closely to the combat zone of their homes."[12] A symphony of sorrows is being composed by a generation of musicians still struggling with the scars from divorces decades old. Blink 182, Everclear, Go Fish, FFH, Korn, Lifehouse, Linkin Park, Nickelback, Papa Roach, Pink, Slipknot, Staind, Tait, and countless others speak in eloquent song to voice the hurts of a broken generation.

For too long we have debated without representation. In an effort to calm our parents' consciences, we've been urged to suffer in silence. Society's unspoken expectation is that we should just "get over it." Things could be much worse, you know. "Lots of parents divorce," we're told, as if the commonality of our pain lessens the severity of it. To tell us, "You're a mature kid; you'll be fine," is like telling the NFL player out with a career-ending injury the week before his first Super Bowl, "It's okay; you can still watch the game."

Negating our devastation is as destructive as ignoring it. Divorce *hurts.* Rather than acknowledge how divorce has affected us, society asks us to be nice and put up with the consequences of it. Bob, whose parents divorced when he was eleven, laments, "I hated my stepmom because she was the one that broke up my family. And yet I had to visit and eat turkey and mashed potatoes with her and always treat her as if she were an old friend of the family." Oddly enough, it was often *our* failure to accept such changes that marked us as truly troubled. But why shouldn't we be troubled by the breakup of our homes? Just because our voices weren't heard (or acknowledged) doesn't mean that our questions didn't exist.

Divorce is hard on *any* child, at *any* age. We need the stability of our parents for our entire lives. Our folks don't give up their parenting role simply because we have left home. We still look to our parents to guide us and affirm us through life decisions such as settling on our college major, deciding where to live, making career choices, selecting a spouse, and raising our own children. Those of us whose parents divorced when we were young may grow up with holes in our histories because events, if they can be recalled at all, may be tainted with bitterness or rage. And those of us who were eighteen or older when our parents divorced share the issues of self-doubt and fear of intimacy but have the additional guilt of wondering if our parents sacrificed happiness in life because of us. All we knew turned out to be a facade. And if we're married—especially to someone just like Mom or Dad—we fear we're destined to divorce as well. We may seem happy now, but the other shoe will eventually drop.

For *adult* children of divorce frustrated with a lack of support for their grief, I offer this analogy: Imagine you are putting together a puzzle and have only a few pieces left when someone comes in and knocks over the table, scattering all the pieces to the floor. Does the fact that you were almost done lessen the frustration you feel over having to start over? The pain of those who experience parental divorce when they are adults is often downplayed. The truth is that divorce is still a major setback because, as you start to reassemble your work, you find that the picture you have been studying has changed. Each puzzle piece must be re-examined to see if it still fits the photo of your memory. While those who were young when their parents divorced don't have a picture to compare their puzzle pieces to, adult children of divorce question the validity of their history, their values, and their memories because their foundation has been torn away. After a lifetime of looking up to Mom and Dad and consciously or unconsciously viewing that marriage as a correct picture, they are overwhelmed by the thought that what they once knew as truth has been revealed as a lie.

Responses to divorce may differ, but each divorce is distressing because it represents an unwelcome revision of the way we have come to understand the world.

Why Look Back?

Why is it important to address the issues that arise from our parents' divorce? Because until we have a firm sense of our own past—both good and bad—and begin to heal from it, we won't have a solid foundation for building the future we hope to have. Children of divorce are much like adult adoptees struggling with an unknown past. The adoptee's past is hidden; ours is ignored. The adoptee wrestles with the transition from being unwanted to being chosen. The child of divorce struggles to understand how she can be loved when one or both parents—from her perspective—have abandoned her.

We've been told to accept the divorce as part of our past, but until we acknowledge the feelings and effects of it, we will not be able to break free of our past's power to affect our present and our future. It's easier to ignore or stuff our feelings than it is to express or experience them. This fear of feeling causes us to build walls. In an ongoing effort to regain stability, we try to control our environment. We make those around us jump through hoops, yet we run away from any hoops presented to us. We expect others to love us unconditionally before we remove the conditions from our love. Often, we're blind to the mixed messages we send.

Perhaps you've come to believe that divorce is normal and acceptable. Perhaps you've lowered your expectations as a way to deal with your parents' divorce by telling yourself:

- My marriage will probably fail, so I'll just enjoy it while it lasts.
- The only way I can avoid divorce is to not marry, so I'll live with my significant other instead.
- Even Christians divorce, so why should I follow an outdated tradition of faith?

One thirty-four-year-old doggedly expressed his acceptance of his parents' divorce by saying, "I'm an adult, and I have dealt with it in an adult way. It was not my fault, nor my responsibility. I can't fix it, so I've moved on." While there is truth to his statements, his wife of four years jumped in to tell him, "You have no idea how much the divorce has influenced you and our marriage. You have not dealt with it, and you won't ever talk about it so that we can deal with it. Sometimes I'm not sure if I'm dealing with you as an adult, or if I'm really interacting with a hurt child. I wish I knew so I could help *us*."

No doubt about it, humans are a flawed group. We fail to live up to our own lofty expectations every day. Does that mean we should quit trying? Of course not! The athlete doesn't quit practicing in the midst of pain. He keeps at it because the goal of winning offers more satisfaction than any relief from his present discomfort. A mountain climber is not satisfied with *attempting* to climb Mount Everest. The pleasure comes with reaching the summit. No one who's been married will tell you that the union is easy, but any couple who has celebrated a fiftieth anniversary will testify that the sum of the ebb and flow of marital satisfaction is far more fulfilling than the strain of any particular incident. In fact, it's often through the trials, one might argue, that a marriage is strengthened. Few things are more deeply satisfying than accomplishing that which was thought impossible.

The Love They Lost Versus the Love We Want

Children of divorce are caught between two equally dominant pulls. On the one hand, the love we seek represents all the love and security we lost. On the other hand, the fear of failing at love, or becoming what we despise, immobilizes us. One divorced dad told me that he couldn't understand why his son would remain married in a situation that made him so obviously miserable. His son had spent the twenty-some years after his parents' divorce trying to be all the things he perceived his father was not. If his marriage failed, in his mind, he would become just like his dad. It was easier to stay in an unhappy marriage than face the possibility of empathizing with his dad and the decision he made years before.

Stephanie Staal crafted an excellent collage of our collective conscience in her book *The Love They Lost: Living with the Legacy of Our
Parents' Divorce*. Where Wallerstein's book is objective, Staal's is personal.
Where Wallerstein observes, Staal reflects. Again, familiar themes surface
as a hundred voices unite: Divorce defines our identity. Divorce morphs
the cement of stability into the sand of uncertainty. Divorce skews our
understanding of bedrock concepts such as home, family, and love. And
once again, the effects of our parents' divorce fully impact us when we
pursue our own romantic relationships because, as Staal explains, "We
knew too much about how relationships end before our own relationships
have even started."[13]

Affirming the idea that divorce is never a dead issue, she concludes:

> How do I write a conclusion to a story that is still unfolding for
> so many of us, including me? I don't have a perfect ending to
> offer you. My parents still make unpleasant remarks and intima-
> tions about each other. I still have to figure out where I'm going
> to spend my holidays. I still haven't put on a white dress and
> walked down the aisle, moved by a renewed faith in love. I still
> wonder, if I ever have children, will their grandparents be able to
> sit together in the same room? I still feel twinges of sadness at the
> oddest moments, and I still have an armful of memories that hurt
> when I squeeze them.[14]

Moving Beyond the Legacy of Our Past

While it's true that we will continue to wrestle with the impact of divorce
throughout our life, as Christians we are not alone in our struggle, and we
have access to Someone who can offer us wisdom and healing as we seek
to change our involuntary inheritance.

It wasn't until twenty-five years after my mom and dad's divorce that

I had this epiphany: I am choosing to derive my identity from a past event over which I had no control, when God is offering me the opportunity to choose an identity that affirms my future with Him!

Exodus 34:6-7 reads:

> I am the LORD, the merciful and gracious God. I am slow to anger and rich in unfailing love and faithfulness. I show this unfailing love to many thousands by forgiving every kind of sin and rebellion. Even so I do not leave sin unpunished, but I punish the children for the sins of their parents to the third and fourth generations. (NLT)

Our prayers are echoed in Psalm 79:8:

> Do not hold against us the sins of the fathers; may your mercy come quickly to meet us, for we are in desperate need.

Though it isn't popular to admit, divorce is sin. It is—like all sin—a decision that places a wedge between God and sinner, and must be confessed to restore spiritual intimacy. Our parents' decision to divorce was sinful, but it is—like all sin—forgivable. God is compassionate and gracious. He forgives all who seek to be forgiven. However, while forgiveness affects the eternal ramifications of our sins, it does not necessarily take away the earthly consequences of our choices. Divorce is a prominent example of generational sin. As with alcoholism and other hereditary tendencies, our parents passed down to us the propensity to divorce. Statistics tell us that without intentional intervention—taking action to learn different patterns of relating—we are likely to follow in our parents' footsteps.

As adults we are now responsible for our own choices. Simply stomping our feet and saying, "I will *not* get divorced!" is not enough. As my friend Heather so clearly articulates, "If children who are from dysfunctional homes don't set out to learn how to handle things differently, they are almost certain to re-create the only situation they've ever known." If we grew up with insecurity, instability, and chaos, we may inadvertently use those characteristics to sabotage healthy relationships because those are the traits for which we have developed coping mechanisms.

Instead of living our life in response to our past, we can choose to go to God for healing and to live our life in anticipation of the future He promises us. Millions of us share the experience of divorce. While the deck may seem stacked against us, we have the ultimate wild card. As Christians, we have a permanent place in our Abba Father's family. His love for us is unconditional. His resources are unending, and His faithfulness is unfailing. We have been gifted with unique talents, abilities, and passions. We have been created with a purpose. Our family is as broad as the millions of fellow believers around the world and as specific as the mentors we adopt and the accountability groups we form. Love has been perfectly personified in Jesus Christ. Through His offer of adoption, we are able to discover hope and find home as Abba's children.

Are you ready to begin the healing process? Step one is making peace...

Word

And we know that in all things God works for the good of those who love him, who have been called according to his purpose.
(Romans 8:28)

Reflect

- How many of your friends are children of divorced parents?
- Did you ever feel that you were missing out on what others had because of your parents' divorce? Give an example.

- Was there a particular event that illustrated to you that your parents' divorce was still affecting your life as an adult? Describe it.
- If you were asked to introduce yourself and your life in fifty words, what would you say?
- What challenges have you faced in establishing your own relationships?
- Spend some time reflecting on the thoughts and memories that resurfaced as you read this chapter. Be specific.
- What do you hope to gain from reading this book?

Challenge

Select a book from the reading list below. As you read it, allow memories to surface. Capture them in your journal.

Read

The Divorce Culture by Barbara Dafoe Whitehead (Knopf, 1997)

The Unexpected Legacy of Divorce by Judith S. Wallerstein and Sandra Blakeslee (Hyperion, 2000)

The Love They Lost: Living with the Legacy of Our Parents' Divorce by Stephanie Staal (Delacorte Press, 2000)

Split: Stories from a Generation Raised on Divorce by Ava Chin (Contemporary Books, 2002)

Make Peace

Effect: The experience of divorce hinders our ability to genuinely forgive others, especially our parents.

Hope: We can choose to release resentment and develop the ability to forgive.

In *The Secret of Loving,* Josh McDowell wrote that resolving a conflict is more rewarding than dissolving a relationship.[1] This is especially true when it comes to making peace with our parents and the impact of divorce on our life. Making peace doesn't mean that we like the impact of the divorce or that we condone or accept it as good. It does mean that we acknowledge it, grieve it, and choose our response to it. We make peace with our pasts when we decide not to react to the present based on past experiences and hurts, but rather choose to respond in ways that enhance the futures we desire.

Making peace means we choose to accept our parents for who they are today, with all of their imperfections and the consequences of their choices. While we're quick to acknowledge that our own emotions and moods fluctuate, we tend to forget that our relationships ebb and flow as well. Making peace in our relationships does not mean we'll live in perpetual bliss. It does mean we choose to forgive and accept forgiveness, release resentment, and commit to the continuation of a relationship—in whatever form it may need to take—rather than walk away from a burned bridge.

I learned this lesson firsthand when things came to a head between my mom and me the summer I was eighteen. My mom and my stepdad were already separated, and I was home alone one night when a situation developed that was dangerous to me. In a panic, I packed up my car and fled. A few months later, before leaving for college, I returned in the quiet of the night to drop off a harsh, disapproving note for my mom. The note explained her responsibility for the situation that led me to flee and force-fully let her know I no longer wanted a relationship with her. It was the last willing communication I would have with her for a long time.

In the months between graduation and my first day of college, I stayed with friends, rented a room above a bar, and even stayed with my dad for a few weeks. In doing the latter, I became keenly aware of how successfully my father had created a new family with his new wife and four new kids. At a time when I needed the security of home and the love of family, I had neither. I left for college feeling utterly alone, forgotten, and replaced.

I struggled that first semester as the reality and ramifications of my mom and stepdad's divorce set in. In addition to suffering emotional despondency, I was hard-pressed financially. My aid was based on Mom and John's combined income. Mom didn't know for sure where I was, and I didn't want to want anything from her. I didn't feel I had a right to ask Dad for money because he was the "at home" dad to four other kids. My relationship with John confused me. Since he was not my biological father, he no longer had any financial obligation to me. Even though John had raised me from age seven to eighteen, I sensed that Mom's divorce of John was John's divorce of me.

Alone with my indignation and financial frustrations, I chose bitter-ness. I clung to it as my right and allowed it to envelop me. Life had let me down, and on some level I believed that to let go of my seething bit-terness would be to agree that I was as worthless and disposable as I felt.

I wanted to be happy, but I no longer knew how to choose that emo-tion. I convinced myself that I was better off without my family. Ironically, in choosing to react to my pain in that way, I was actually making my parents the center of my life. Every decision and every thought revolved around my goal of proving to myself that I didn't need them.

If you had met me during this time, you likely would not have seen this side of me. You would have perceived that I was a hard worker as I balanced four jobs with my full course schedule. You would have seen me as studious as I maintained a high GPA to retain my scholarships and grants. You might have thought I was a little snobbish because I didn't socialize very much. The truth was, I didn't have any money to spend and feared for my future if I failed to make my tuition payments.

Though I appeared successful and fairly well adjusted, I felt empty and dissatisfied. I could never let down, or my parents would "win." I didn't want to need anyone, least of all them. If I didn't need anyone, no one could hurt me, or so I thought. Self-sufficiency was my goal.

In addition to my academic pursuits, I began to explore my spirituality in order to make sense of the pain and confusion in my life. My hope was to find a self-reliant religion—one that didn't require dependence on anyone or anything. I wanted the freedom to pick and choose what to believe. What I discovered was that this type of religion was no faith at all. It was just a simple rationalization to justify doing whatever I wanted. And it didn't do anything to take away the ache in my heart.

During this time, I met a woman who seemed to be at peace with her life, and I desperately wanted what she had. As a result of our friendship, I began to reexamine the claims of Christianity. I discovered that Christianity is the only faith in which God—or any divine force—reaches out to us, accepts us as we are, and then enables us to improve our lives as a result of His work in us. All other belief systems are based on the idea that we must first change ourselves or control ourselves in a vain attempt to make ourselves acceptable to the deity. Christianity offers unconditional love, an identity-defining purpose, and a promise of a permanent home—everything I ever wanted.

After deciding to follow Christ, I developed relationships with other

Christians who encouraged me to choose God's ways over my own stubborn will. But whenever my friends expressed concern about my hardened attitude toward my family, I brushed them off, defending the uniqueness of my situation. Surely it was better to walk away than try to find a way to fit into my mixed-up family. And give up my rage? No way!

But over time, everything I read, every sermon I heard, every conversation I had seemed divinely arranged to prove me wrong. Even the radio pricked my conscience! Mike + the Mechanics' "In the Living Years" drove me to nightmares as I wondered what my future would be like if I didn't make amends before death took away my opportunity.

Though I had maintained a weak connection with my dad and stepdad, I had not communicated with my mom since the night I left home. Even as a new Christian, I knew I could not maintain my hate. Nearly a year of silence passed before I finally broke down and called her. I didn't call expecting my mom to apologize. Instead, I asked her to forgive me for hating her. It wasn't an easy conversation, or even a long one. It was awkward and went against every emotion I felt. But I knew I had done the right thing. That night I slept well for the first time in a long, long time.

Though I felt relief, I did not experience the overwhelming release I wanted. I had not realized how much my bitterness had become a part of me and that it could not vanish completely as a result of one short, stilted phone call. I made the decision to forgive that night, but it took years for my feelings to follow. Because my mom did not apologize for hurting me, I constantly struggled to relinquish the resentment I felt justified to maintain. It took a long time to realize that her remorse could not be a prerequisite to my forgiveness. I continued to guard my heart from further pain, and over time our trust was rebuilt in safe, baby steps.

Our parents may have made some wrong or hurtful choices. In the midst of taking care of themselves, they may have forgotten to take care of us. Without their protective cover, we were hurt, perhaps even abused. In reality, our parents did wrong us, and we will pay the consequences of their actions for the rest of our lives. However, regardless of our pasts, we each have a choice: Will I allow my pain to make me bitter toward my parents, or will I take responsibility for my own choices and choose to make peace instead?

DYSFUNCTION DESTRUCTED

There's no such thing as a perfect family. Each family will fall short of the perfect ideal God intended and thus be dysfunctional.

We may not even be aware of how we are allowing our families' dysfunctions to influence our treatment of others. After my mom and stepdad's divorce, I shut out my family because, from my perspective, I could gain nothing by putting myself back in the middle of their fragmented fray. Even though my parents' divorce was final, their mutual resentment and bitter innuendoes still surfaced, and I didn't want to be a filter for those feelings. I was hurt because, at a time when I needed them, they were too absorbed with their own problems. Overwhelmed and unable to adjust to all the changes, I opted out.

What I didn't realize was that my decision to disengage from my family hurt me just as much as my parents' decision to divorce. Perhaps the degrees of hurtful severity were unequal, but the hardness of my heart that resulted from my segregation rendered me incapable of the love I was so angry to have been denied. I have talked with many adult children of divorce who have had similar experiences, including Kris.

Kris' father left home when she was only a year old, and he never looked back. Her mom never remarried, never dated. Kris grew up with a model of family that didn't include a man. As an adult, Kris didn't have much interest in dating until her mom died suddenly. Faced with the prospect of growing old alone, Kris grudgingly began to date.

At twenty-seven and on the brink of engagement to Eric, Kris found herself fending off explosive emotions she couldn't understand. The couple wisely sought counseling and, in doing so, discovered that Kris didn't have a working model of what a husband should be. When Eric would talk about marriage, his dreams, instead of evoking romantic desire, filled Kris with fear and apprehension. She couldn't picture a future with Eric because she didn't understand the roles he was hoping to play. The couple put off their marriage plans to focus on helping Kris make peace with her past, forgive the father she hadn't met, and develop a healthy model of marriage and family.

How, then, can we make peace with our families? We begin by taking time to grieve our losses.

GRIEVING OUR LOSSES

As a college student, I began to see that underneath my rage, burrowed under that bitterness, festering under my fears, were intense sadness and loss. As I've talked with other adult children of divorce, I've discovered that these feelings are universal. As children of divorce, we experience incredible loss: the loss of stability, the loss of financial security, the loss of continuity, the loss of shared history, and the loss of deep intimacy with both parents. Sometimes we lose even the freedom to express this feeling of loss. We also experience a loss of innocent trust when it comes to love and marriage. We may listen to a friend in love with a jaded ear because we doubt love that unconditional can last. We may sabotage or avoid romantic relationships because we don't know how to recognize healthy love. And even as we shake our head at our parents' idealistic naiveté, we are just as quixotic if we believe that sheer desire alone will prevent us from becoming another statistic. We have some hard work to do first.

Before we can have peaceful hearts, we must grieve our disappointments and hurts. We must give ourselves permission to let the tears flow. Perhaps we see tears as an indication of weakness or a loss of control, and we want nothing more than to be strong and self-sufficient. Understand that grief comes in waves. We can't "get over" our loss in one or two crying sessions. We may grieve for years as new experiences reveal new losses—and that's okay. When feelings of sadness overwhelm us, we need to let ourselves feel them. The only way to deal with loss is to go through it.

Perhaps you've become so good at stuffing your hurts that you can't even access them to express them. Try these suggestions for getting in touch with emotions you may have suppressed:

- Take a tour of your history. Page through your parents' wedding pictures, whether the album has been dismantled or not. Try to imagine what your life would be like if they had remained in the love they felt that day.
- Watch an old home video and consider what was really going on behind the scenes.
- Take a drive through your old neighborhood. Bring your journal with you and write down as many memories as you can.
- Try to find mementos from your parents' marriage: wedding rings, the topper from their wedding cake, Christmas decorations, photo albums, or anything else that symbolizes the sentiment of family for you.
- Listen to songs popular at the time of the divorce or written from the experience of divorce.[2]

In addition, try writing out your answers to the following questions:

- How did you learn about your parents' intention to divorce?
- Why, to the best of your knowledge, did your parents divorce? Do you agree with this reasoning? Do you think the divorce was a good decision for them? for you?
- Have you ever had a conversation with either of your parents about the marriage and divorce? If so, how old were you? Try to record that conversation now.
- How do you think your parents' divorce has affected your life for better and/or for worse?

- Have either of your parents remarried? How has that affected you?
- Who do you consider your immediate family now? Are you at peace with this arrangement?
- Have you come to a place of peace about your past? If so, how have you reached that point? If not, what is holding you back?

The purpose of this exercise is not to wallow in the hurts of the past but to release the hurt inside of you so that your heart will soften. My prayer is that you will begin to understand that resentment and bitterness hold you prisoner to your hurt. You will never be free to move ahead and create different patterns unless you make peace with your parents and the consequences of their divorce on your life.

As we begin to grieve our losses, we can also seek to better understand our parents.

Learning from Our Parents' Own Hurts and History

We can develop more compassion and grace toward our parents if we seek to understand the experiences that shaped them and the motivations that led them to do the things they did. Sometimes our parents' personal problems led to their divorce. Hurting people hurt people. No surprise there.

There was a time when I felt that understanding my parents meant knowing all the details about their past. I thought that if I could analyze every aspect of the breakdown of their marriages, I could figure out the secret to avoiding divorce. My pastor helped me see that God could heal me and help me discover what I was looking for in life without my knowing all the sordid details of the demise of my parents' marriages.

Regardless of the reasons behind our parents' divorce, it is unlikely that they want us to repeat their experience. As time passes and their hearts heal, consider approaching your parents for an honest reflection on their failed marriage. Before doing so, though, take some time to pray about the timing. Just as we find it difficult to speak with our parents regarding the impact of their divorce, our parents might think the topic is too private or intrusive or condemning to discuss with us.

We have a right to know as much about our pasts as our parents are willing to share, but we must remember that the past cannot be changed. At best, we can learn from it. As Stephanie Staal wrote, "It seems sort of ridiculous, our refusal to speak of an event that had such an influence in shaping our lives."[3] A natural part of the maturation process—regardless of our family structure—is being able to look at what our parents taught us, both implicitly and intentionally, and then decide for ourselves which traditions to continue and which to change.

If you feel a green light to approach your parents, set aside a time to broach the subject. This list is an adaptation of the questions I used when I talked with each of my parents and my stepdad. Feel free to add or adjust to fit your own situation.

1. What qualities attracted you to Mom (Dad)?
2. What made you decide to marry?
3. Why do you think your marriage broke up?
4. In what ways did you think leaving Mom (Dad) was a good decision for you?
5. Do you still think it was the best decision?
6. Do you have any regrets? What would you do differently?
7. What was the best thing about being married to Mom (Dad)?
8. What was the hardest?
9. What surprised you most about marriage?
10. What do you wish you had known before you decided to get married?
11. What were some of the significant life-shaping events in your life, and what impact did those events have on your personality and ability to be a good spouse?
12. How do you think the divorce has affected your ability to parent me?

13. What do you want me to learn from your mistakes?
14. How would you feel if I got divorced?
15. Drawing on your experience, what advice would you give me on love, marriage, and parenting?

All three conversations provided an incredible means of connection for my parents and me. They were able to better understand how their decisions affected me, and I had an opportunity to learn from their mistakes. Most helpful to me was that for the first time I remember, they acknowledged my pain and perspective.

My time with my stepdad was especially meaningful. Because he is not my biological father, John and I had never talked about our post-divorce relationship. I think it was probably pretty difficult for him to separate his feelings for me from his divorce of my mom. By the time the dust had settled and Mom and John were ready to resume their relationships with me, I had become accustomed to being alone. With John, the struggle to maintain our relationship intensified when he remarried. His response to me was alternately hot and cold. One year he'd remember my birthday, the next year he wouldn't.

My conversation with John about his and Mom's marriage and divorce, and its impact on me, was very healing for both of us. He admitted two things to me that no one had affirmed before, though I knew them to be true. He acknowledged that he and Mom broke an important promise to me, and he admitted that I was forgotten in the midst of a very bitter divorce. This conversation was a turning point for me. Though we still don't see or talk to each other very much, I no longer wonder whether he cares, and I have a better understanding of what happened and why.

In talking with each of my parents, I sought understanding, not affirmation or even acknowledgment of the hurt they had caused me. I encourage you to approach your parents without any expectations regarding their response; instead seek to get to know them better and to affirm their hurts and history. In doing so, you may create the environment where their acknowledgment of your hurt occurs.

CHOOSING FORGIVENESS

We become more willing to forgive our parents when we acknowledge that we all mess up. We all hurt others, and we're all in desperate and utter need of Someone larger than ourselves to help us rise above our own humanity. The solution is not normalizing our sin—or our parents'—it is confessing our own and forgiving theirs.

God knows we cannot live perfect lives, so He provided the perfect way for us to deal with our imperfections. He gave us a Peacemaker who could forgive us and model for us how to forgive others.

As children of divorce, we have learned to live with loss. We might have felt neglected, abandoned, unloved, and uncared for. That may have been true for a season, but God went to extravagant lengths to illustrate the depth of His sacrificial love for us. Long before we were born, God's Son took the rap for not only our misdeeds, but the hurts our parents caused us as well. Jesus didn't deserve death, and we don't deserve God's grace. Yet God so longs to be a part of our life that He allowed His own Son to die to make room for us in His family. If this kind of love is a new concept for you, I encourage you to turn to the invitation in appendix A to learn how you can become a part of God's family.

So here's the million-dollar question: How can we forgive our parents? The answer lies in our understanding of grace. Our heart can only express that which it contains. If we are filled with bitterness, how can we expect to demonstrate love and forgiveness? Brennan Manning wrote, "For experiencing God's love in Jesus Christ means experiencing that one has been unreservedly accepted, approved and infinitely loved."[4] We must first ask

God to forgive us and fill our heart with love. Then, from the overflow of that love, we can act lovingly toward others. When we accept our own need for God's forgiveness, we can then, in gratitude, extend forgiveness to others.

"But," you may say, "if I forgive someone, does that mean I have to let that person walk all over me? Doesn't that send the message that I'm okay with what they did? Does that mean I have to let them back in to wreak havoc on my life?" Forgiveness is an especially delicate subject when it comes to our families because many of the hurts that need forgiving are ongoing. As Gary Chapman, ex-husband to singer Amy Grant, said in an interview, "Divorce is the funeral that never ends."[5] But it will do your

Releasing Resentment

1. *Stop.* When you catch yourself feeling bitter or resentful, stop and commit yourself to living at peace with others.

2. *Consider.* Resentment feeds off the bile of bitterness. Speaking negatively about another is a gourmet feast.

3. *Commit.* Commit yourself to refrain from saying anything that would cause a bystander to think negatively about your offender.

4. *Remember.* Remind yourself of the objective: "Make every effort to live in peace with all men and to be holy; without holiness no one will see the Lord. See to it that no one misses the grace of God and that no bitter root grows up to cause trouble and defile many" (Hebrews 12:14-15).

5. *Pray.* Ask God to fill your heart with love and a desire to forgive. Ask Him to reveal how you may have contributed to the conflict, and resolve to make amends.

6. *Confess.* Bitterness and resentment reveal that we think someone is beyond the reach of God's grace and that Christ's death was not enough to cover all sins (most notably those of the one

heart a world of good if you focus on reconciliation rather than rationalization of your rage.

Many of us became bitter or jaded or guarded because our parents did not fulfill the expectation we had for them to stay together. When our families dissolved, so did our resolve to love unconditionally, trust unguardedly, live fully. But regardless of how others have hurt us or allowed us to hurt, we must forgive if we want to honor God and heal from our pasts.

To be absolutely blunt, if we harbor resentment or a desire for revenge, we are appointing ourself to a position that only Christ can claim. We are telling God that we know better than He how to impart

who offended us). Ask God's forgiveness for your bitterness.

7. *Ponder.* Think of three good things about the person who hurt you. Say them aloud, write them down, or tell a friend.

8. *Intercede.* Pray for the best interest of the other. A good test of the purity of your prayer is to ask yourself if you would pray those same things for yourself. A suggested start: Pray for a new or renewed relationship with Christ, pray for closer intimacy in marriages and other relationships, pray for success in work, pray for wisdom to make right choices.

9. *Confide.* Ask someone you respect to hold you accountable to releasing your resentment. Make a habit of naming three positive traits about the person you resent, then ask your friend to pray with you for him or her. (In some cases, it may be wise to seek the assistance of a counselor as part of this process as well.)

10. *Forgive.* Prayer is a means of spiritual connection. As your heart softens toward that person, be open to renewing the relationship if it is possible to do so without opening yourself up to additional hurt.

justice. The fact is, our parents are not accountable to us for their actions; they are accountable to God. As much good as it does our heart to hear them acknowledge the hurt their choices have caused us, unless we have a willingness to forgive them, our healing will be incomplete.

Forgiveness Defined

The word *forgive* conjures up a multitude of meanings. The *Random House College Dictionary, Revised Edition* defines it this way:

1. to grant full pardon for or remission of (an offense, debt, etc.)
2. to give up all claim on account of
3. to grant free pardon to (a person)
4. to cease to feel resentment against
5. to pardon an offense or an offender

In other words, to forgive means to cancel a debt, to release an offense without exacting a penalty, and most important, to cease to feel resentment against the offender. Forgiveness means accepting someone as is, with his or her faults and whether or not the person asks for forgiveness. It is making an intentional choice to release resentment. This goes utterly and completely against our human nature, but it is the only option for those who want peaceful hearts.

Just to make things perfectly clear, here are a few truths about forgiveness:

- *Forgiveness is a choice.* We can't choose our past, but we can choose how to respond to past events. Forgiveness is the way we choose to move on.
- *Forgiveness is between you and God, not you and the offender.* Some make the offender's request for forgiveness a condition to their granting it. Because sin by its very nature is an offense against God, He is the One who is responsible for exacting the consequences of that sin. When we forgive, we pass our hurt to Him.

- *Forgiveness is a response, not an approval.* You may be thinking, *How can I let go?* When we condone something, we are saying it's okay. When we forgive, we choose not to hold a grudge. We extend forgiveness in response to our grasp of grace in our own lives.
- *Forgiveness doesn't mean the offense never happened.* The offender will still suffer consequences, either here or hereafter, but that is between the offender and God.
- *Forgiveness reveals the character of one's heart.* As believers, we are the recipients of God's undeserved favor and love. As we grow in faith, we grow in our ability to submit our wills to God's, and our characters better mirror His.
- *Forgiveness is unconditional.* You can't accept God's grace and not share it with others. Once you forgive, you cannot take it back.
- *Forgiveness doesn't define the other by his or her offense.* You forfeit the right to associate the offense with the offender. You are not the same person you were a year ago. You have made errors in moments of passion. You have learned from your mistakes. If you want to grow, you must allow others the same freedom.
- *Forgiveness isn't fair.* Forgiveness is about grace, not justice.
- *Forgiveness is a partnership with God in grace.* We might think we need to be able to forgive fully before we can extend grace, but we need only to be willing to let go. God will do the rest. It will take time for our feelings to follow, but we can remind ourselves that feelings are not fact. In faith, make the decision to forgive with the acknowledgment that it is the first, most difficult step.
- *Forgiveness is a way of life.* We will continue to be hurt and to hurt others for the rest of our life. When we embrace grace, we better bear the image of the Christ we claim.

Submitting to God and choosing to forgive our parents for their divorce and the ways they have hurt us is hard work. It will take time and intentional effort, not only because it goes against what we've been shown, but because it goes against our human nature. The world may wonder at our ways, but we have been given an amazing responsibility. As members of God's family, we have become His ambassadors to a world that will see in our lives a personified message of the reality of reconciliation.

Word

Be kind and compassionate to one another, forgiving each other, just as in Christ God forgave you. (Ephesians 4:32)

Reflect

- What are some of the losses you've had to mourn (or will mourn) as a result of your parents' divorce? Think about your home, your sense of stability and belonging, specific rituals and traditions, financial implications, shared history, and the depth of relationship you have with your parents.
- How do you think your life would be different (for better and worse) if your parents had worked out their differences? How does that comparison make you feel about your life as it is now?
- Consider this statement: *Forgiveness means refusing to continue to bear a grudge against another person. One way to test your feelings of forgiveness is to ask yourself if you tend to give this person the benefit of the doubt or if you assume that his or her future behavior will match the prior offense.* Is there anyone in your life about whom it is a struggle to assume the best?
- Based on your previous answers, do you think you need to make any changes in your life? If so, list them.
- Have you forgiven your parents for their divorce? If yes, do they know?
- Is there someone to hold you accountable as you work toward

forgiving your parents? It might be helpful for that person to read this chapter, especially the steps for releasing resentment on pages 38–39.

• Make a list of any and all persons against whom you hold a grudge. List each person's name and the grudge you bear against that individual. When you're finished, write:

I am choosing to hold resentment against these people (this person). I have determined that what they have done in the past is worse than any good that they could do in the future. Jesus' death may have covered my sin, but it wasn't enough to cover theirs. Therefore, in my mind, I will always look at them through the lens of my hurt.

If this entry makes you squirm, GREAT! Your conscience is convicting you, and you are ready to release your resentment. Now write each person's name and the grudge you've held again. This time, underneath each one, write this:

I acknowledge that ———— [name] hurt me when he/she did ———— [grudge]. I also acknowledge that I may have contributed to the problem by ————. I now recognize that both ———— [name] and I are flawed humans who do hurtful and mean things. I choose to release the resentment I have been feeling against ———— [name]. Although it's still hard for me to seek the good, I can say that he/she has these three good qualities: (1) ————, (2) ————, and (3) ————. The next time I see this person, I will choose to focus on these things. I am going to ask ———— [another name] to now keep me accountable for seeking the good in ———— [name] and praying for his/her best interest.

Challenge

Ask your parents if they would be willing to allow you to talk with them about their divorce and its impact on you. It may help to keep your emotions in check if you and your parent assume the roles of interviewer and interviewee respectively. Record the conversation for future listening.

Read

> *Secrets of Your Family Tree: Healing for Adult Children of Dysfunctional Families* by Dave Carder (Moody, 1991)
>
> *In the Grip of Grace* by Max Lucado (W Publishing, 1996)
>
> *Forgiving Our Parents, Forgiving Ourselves* by David Stoop and James Masteller (Vine, 1996)
>
> *What's So Amazing About Grace?* by Philip Yancey (Zondervan, 1997)

Grow in Our Faith

Effect: *The experience of divorce creates a false understanding of the character of God.*

Hope: *We can choose to know God for who He really is.*

W hen I asked several adult children of divorce to tell me who was most like the father they wished they had, they answered, "Bill Cosby." No matter what was going on at home, a generation of kids welcomed *The Cosby Show*'s thirty-minute invitation to be part of a family where Dad was present and engaged in the lives of his kids. He disciplined with love and humor. He cheered Rudy on when she was the "sweet feet" of her football team. He terrorized Vanessa's dates with loving protection. He encouraged Denise to express her personality. He had man-to-man talks with Theo about responsibility and integrity. He was a friend and counselor to Sondra and her husband. How many of us were put to bed on Thursday nights with wistful dreams of being a Cosby kid?

God created us to be cared for by both a mom and a dad, full time, all the time. In our attempts to reconcile our realities with the homes we saw on television, we may have told ourselves—and our parents—that we were okay with the split. We adjusted and compensated and learned to live without what we needed and what God desired for us. We may have grown weary of part-time parents when we had full-time needs, but like miniadults, we told ourselves that we understood the necessity.

The child in us, however, couldn't ignore our need. As our parents assured us of their love, we were confused by what that word meant. Love didn't offer us any guarantees that we would be cared for if we believed that Mom and Dad once loved each other. As a result, our conflicted conscience told us that our needs were secondary to our parents' desires. And as adults, we transferred those qualities to a God we're told is supposed to love us like a father.

The map of life passed down to us is littered with faulty information. Statistics tell us that if we blindly follow in the footsteps of our parents, we ourselves are likely to end up divorced. The good news is that with God's help we can revise that map and design a new route.

To begin this process, we must consider how our family background may affect our ability to understand God as our Father, the foundations of our faith, and the role of our church family.

Who's Your Daddy?

A man from my church recently attended a FamilyLife marriage conference. During one of the huddle times, the men were asked to say the first description that came to mind when they heard the word *father*. My friend eagerly piped up, "encourager." In the group of forty or so men, his was the only positive description. Many of us who felt abandoned or betrayed by our fathers struggle with the idea of God as a loving father.

As children of divorce, our initial understanding of our heavenly Father reflects the relationship we had (or didn't have) with our earthly dads. If the father we can see taught us by his choices that love is fickle, security is temporary, and faithfulness is fleeting, it requires quite a leap of faith to believe that a heavenly Father exists whose love is unconditional, whose security is eternal, and whose faithfulness is unfailing. Perhaps you know the textbook description of God our Father, but when the lonely times come, your emotions don't match the truth you profess.

How often have you struggled to relate to God as Father? The Bible tells us that God Himself steps in to father the fatherless. In Psalm 68:6

we're promised that God sets the lonely in families, and in Psalm 27:10 we're assured that "even if my father and mother abandon me, the LORD will hold me close" (NLT).

Even if your earthly parents failed to love you as you needed to be loved, your heavenly Father longs for you to know that:

- He chooses to cherish you. (See Colossians 3:12.)
- His love for you is sacrificial. (See Romans 5:8 and 1 John 3:16.)
- He has plans for you—plans for good and not for evil. (See Jeremiah 29:11.)
- He doesn't leave you when the outlook is bleak. (See Psalm 23:4.)
- He always has your best interest at heart. He'll bring good even out of the hard times. (See Romans 8:28.)
- He makes you a priority. Your concerns matter to him. (See Psalm 34:15.)

If you are like me and many of the adult children of divorce I know, you might not really *feel* these promises. We have learned to see love—including God's love—as inconsistent, and we'll never be secure in the love offered us until we believe that God is who He says He is. We can begin to change our view of love by spending time with our Abba Father and getting to know Him for who He is. As we grow closer to God, we will learn to trust Him and receive His love. Despite our natural inclination to make our understanding of God fit what we assume of Him based on our earthly parents, by studying God's Word we can create a new paradigm for our understanding of "father."

Growing Up Fatherless is rooted in Mike Nappa's experience as a child of divorce and illustrates the security he found as he embraced his adoption as God's son. He wrote:

> [Late one night I was] trying to figure out why other kids had dads, and I didn't. Finally, my mother said words that have stuck with me the rest of my life.

"Mikey," she said, "you may not have an earthly father, but you do have a Heavenly Father. And He's always there, no matter what."

I didn't fully understand what that meant until years later when, as a sixteen-year-old, I became a Christian myself. But after that, whenever I felt the hole that divorce had put in my life, I remembered my mother's words and threw myself deep into the arms of God. I found He was always there.

When I graduated from high school, my father wasn't there. But my Father was.

When I went across the country to attend college, my father didn't drop me off at school and make sure I was all settled in before he left. But my Father was with me the whole time.

On my wedding day, my father stayed at home. But my Father stood with me at the altar and viewed the beauty that would be my wife coming down the aisle.

When I graduated from college, my father was nowhere to be found. But my Father cheered and smiled as I walked across the stage to receive my diploma.

When my son was born, my father didn't come to rejoice with me. But in the maternity ward at the hospital, my Father wrapped his arms around both me and my son, welcoming my child into the world.[1]

While this chapter focuses on the influence of a father on our faith and parenting perspective, I don't want to overlook the importance of a mother's role. God's design was for us to experience the nurturing guidance of both a mom and a dad, both of whom reflect aspects of God's character. Regardless of which parent raised us, as children of divorce, we are susceptible to giving in to the temptation of downplaying the need and plan for two parents.

How Did the Divorce Affect Your Theology?

In the same way that our parents' divorce may have hindered our understanding of God, the divorce may also have tainted our ability to have a realistic understanding of our faith.

A divorce is especially hard to stomach when our parents raised us to believe that divorce was not an option. In a classic case of "do as I say, not as I do," divorce was the wrong that went against all that our Christian parents told us was right. All the family devotions, Sunday-school lessons, and youth group truths went out the window when Mom and Dad went their separate ways. Yet, each of us needs to find faith for ourselves. Christianity is about a relationship that never ends with One who promises to sustain us, rather than abandon us, when the going gets rough.

The fact that our fathers and mothers failed to keep their marriage together hindered our ability to see the intended symbolism of their union. God created marriage to put skin on His offer of love and reconciliation. Jesus used the analogy of a bride and groom to convey the relationship God has with His church.

Despite misunderstandings and moodiness, two people in marriage are supposed to honor their commitment to love unconditionally, putting the other's needs before their own. If our parents demonstrated that there are limits to forgiveness, how can we believe that God does not maintain those same limitations? Even if our parents had a reasonably amicable divorce, we are still left with the uncomfortable conclusion that not everyone deserves to be loved.

Divorce skews our understanding of biblical truth because our context for interpretation is different. Elizabeth Marquardt has been studying this phenomenon. In an online article, she related:

> At a Protestant seminary one student whose parents were divorced
> told me that the parable of the Prodigal Son held little resonance

for her.[2] She said, "I was always kind of the dutiful one—the one traveling distances to be sure I saw my father." She had friends for whom the story meant a great deal because "they feel like they've gone away and rejected their families and come back. But my family didn't even give me anything to reject. There wasn't a stable enough thing to go away from or come back to."

An evangelical Christian told me that he sees his father in the role of the Prodigal Son, leaving the family to seek his own fortune elsewhere. The child of divorce saw himself in the role of the father, waiting at the doorway for his loved one to return.[3]

How Do You View the Church?

A less obvious effect of divorce on our faith is its impact on our understanding of the church as our adopted family. Because we did not see a working example of reconciliation and restoration demonstrated within the context of our own home, with those we knew, we are wary of believing that those in the church—strangers!—would love and accept us. We have adjusted to a split allegiance, understanding that Mom (and her partner) fulfill some of our needs and Dad (and his partner), with some overlap, fulfill others. In fact, when it comes to our church involvement, we may unconsciously re-create this same scenario. We have normalized our need to avoid putting all our emotional eggs in one familial basket.

I became aware of this tendency in my own life when, eleven years into my journey of faith, I realized that I had never become fully engaged in *one* church body. I never wanted to make a commitment to anyone or anything without a certainty that I could maintain my obligation. I didn't want to let my church down by failing to remain committed to it, yet by not committing, I was actually doing more to avoid fulfilling my responsibility.

Even when I had taken membership steps at one church body, I always had at least a partial allegiance to another. I might attend my "home" church but then participate in the singles group of another or get involved in a small group at another. Not until I was thirty did I decide to change the pattern and fully embrace my chosen church family.

As Generation Ex matures and returns to the church with our own children, pastors and lay leaders will need to better understand us in order to minister to our needs. The proliferation of divorce has been a conundrum for the church. On the one hand, some equate acknowledging a divorce with condoning the choice. Others have been wooed by the cultural way: Divorce is my right, so don't condemn me! Some refrain from reaching out to children of divorce or even acknowledging their long-term struggles because they fear the wrath of divorced parents who would be convicted by the display of compassion.

Ultimately, though, I think the church in general hasn't met the lifelong needs of children of divorce because it—like the society in which it exists—suffers from a lack of knowledge. The church needs to pursue its calling to become a future-focused family, a defender of the (emotionally and physically) fatherless, and a sanctuary overflowing with the good news of our faith.

As the church comes to appreciate our unique needs, it is my hope that awareness of our struggles and experiences will complement the classes and studies that minister to our parents. Our preengagement and pre-marriage classes need to strip away our false expectations and fill our minds with practical applications of love as a choice and an action, not simply a romantic feeling. They can help engaged couples from all backgrounds consider how their parents' marriages (and divorces) have influenced their own expectations of marriage. Older married couples need to mentor newlyweds with honesty and authenticity, letting them know it's okay to doubt and struggle and even disagree with their spouses. Young couples need assurances that the hard times will pass and that their fulfillment will be richer when they choose to work through their struggles.

Divorce recovery classes can offer more insightful and realistic projections of postdivorce life and the lifelong triggers the entire broken family will face. Empty nesters can be recruited to adopt students and singles who may otherwise spend holidays alone, allow special events to pass by unnoticed, and miss out on the mentoring of a role model for all areas of life. Even Sunday-school teachers can benefit from a better understanding of how the phenomenon of divorce gives us a unique perspective. A friend at my church was taken aback when one of her young students grappled with the Christmas story. She thought he was struggling to understand the virgin birth. His perplexion was more poignant: "Why did God divorce Mary?"

However, each of us can grow in faith, even if we are not part of a church body that seeks to address our specific faith issues as adult children of divorce. Part of the growth process for any believer is to exchange a temporal perspective for an eternal one. As this happens—as God changes our understanding of who He is—our thoughts and actions will become less self-centered and more other-focused. We are God's adopted children, and we can learn new patterns of relating from the One who created us.

DADDY DATES

Any relationship of value can be enhanced through quality time together. By making time with God an intentional part of our days, we grow in our intimacy with Him and our awareness of what pleases Him.

Jesus himself modeled this practice. Luke 5:16 shows us that Jesus withdrew to lonely places and prayed. Shortly before He faced death on our behalf, He went to the Garden of Gethsemane to pray to His Father. If He, the perfect human, saw the need to spend time alone with God, pouring out His heart to Him, how much more do we need to spend time with God? God promises that if we draw near to Him, He will draw near to us (see James 4:8).

If the idea of a daily time with God sounds overwhelming, start with a goal of spending five minutes a day, three times a week, and work your way from there. Don't be too hard on yourself if you aren't consistent at first. I have found that when I set attainable goals for my quiet time, like the one mentioned above, I am more likely to be successful. As a result, I feel encouraged rather than discouraged, and I want to increase my time with God out of desire rather than guilt. God loves you and wants to spend time with you. He wants to hear all about your day. He wants to know your concerns. He wants to be involved in your plans. And He has much He wants to tell you, too, if you'll take time to listen. He is always there, always waiting. We won't find a more trustworthy confidant.

There are lots of ways you can spend your quiet time:

Pray

Did your dad or mom make you feel that what you had to say was important? Your Abba inclines His ear to hear every word you say. Have you ever been afraid to say what you *really* felt because you couldn't predict your parents' response? God already knows your feelings, even better than you do.

Sometimes we act as if we are doing God a favor by editing the intensity of our emotions. We seem to think that if we tone down our feelings, God will be more likely to listen to us. But presenting our thoughts in a "nicer" way doesn't make us more acceptable to God. In fact, when we are less than honest about how we truly feel, we are creating a barrier to the authenticity and intimacy God craves to experience with us. God isn't going anywhere. Our raw emotions won't scare Him away. Rather, they compel Him to draw near to us.

In prayer we can honestly name our feelings in the safest possible place. When we are angry, He quells our rage. When we are hurt, He offers comfort. When we are happy, He rejoices with us. When we are overwhelmed, He shares our burdens, even carries them if we'll ask Him to do so. We don't have to tiptoe around God. No matter what we are feeling, we can run into His open embrace.

A newly married friend of mine (who is also a child of divorce) shared an interesting parallel between prayer and communicating with her husband. At times, she and her husband get caught up in their own plans and neglect to pay attention to each other's needs. Rather than drop hints, my friend crawls in her husband's lap and bluntly declares, "I need affirmation." As Abba's much-loved children, we can approach Him with the same boldness.

I remember the first time I heard someone pray to God as if He were sitting right next to us. My friend explained that prayer is simply a conversation with God. Though He is not visible, He is far from absent. We enter into a relationship with Christ by praying to Him, and we grow in our relationship with Him by continuing to pray.

People pray in so many ways—on paper, silently, quietly, out loud, shouting, alone, with a friend, in a group, at church, with simple words, repeating time-honored standards, as free-flowing conversations, in desperate bursts, eyes closed, eyes open, kneeling, sitting, standing, arms outstretched. The important element is not *how* we pray but *that* we pray. Do you have a long commute? Pray during the drive. Does the morning routine rush by? Say a quick prayer in the shower. If you're not in the habit of praying, don't feel that you have to spend an hour every day on your knees. Start with two minutes on your feet—walking to the car, across campus, to a meeting. No doubt, it is a different kind of conversation than one might have with a friend or family member, but if you don't know what to say, consider the following suggestions.

A.C.T.S.

This classic prayer model uses an acronym to outline four types of prayer:

Adoration: Think about how you would describe the most perfect date you could ever imagine. Does it seem odd to gush about your date's attributes? No, of course not. Adoration recognizes all the wonderful attributes of God.

Confession: As you become aware of ways in which you've missed the mark, tell God you're sorry. Ask Him to forgive you and give you the strength to avoid making the same mistake again. Ask Him to change you so that you respond to circumstances as He would. If your sin affected someone else, ask Him to give you the words to say as you seek that person's forgiveness. If your sin is based in a wrong understanding of yourself, someone else, or God Himself, ask Him to clearly show you the truth.

Thanksgiving: Think of all the ways God has blessed you, then express your gratitude.

Supplication: Supplication is a fancy word for "ask." Tell God your concerns. If you have a decision to make, ask Him for direction. Psalm 32:8 promises, "I will instruct you and teach you in the way you should go; I will counsel you and watch over you." Then read the Bible and seek godly counsel with an open mind. Resist the urge to pray only for yourself. Pray for your family, friends, church, neighbors, government, coworkers, and especially your enemies.

Daily Discussions
Assign a focus for each day (such as church, family, friends, work, and future) and use your commute time for prayer time. For example, I have a note card with each day's focus clipped to the visor of my car. Friday prayers, which are focused on my future, often look like this:

Dear Lord,

I am so grateful that as I wonder about my future, I can also take comfort in the fact that You are more concerned about the details of my life than I am. I thank You for the dreams You have given me— to marry and to have a family someday. I get so impatient waiting for my Mr. Wonderful. To be honest, Lord, sometimes I feel like it's not very important to You. Give me the faith to trust that You will provide Your will in Your time.

I pray that You would ground me in the present even as I antici-pate my future. I ask that You would show me today what I can do to please You and become more like the woman You want me to be. I pray for my future husband and ask that even today You instill in him a desire to be a godly husband and father. I ask that You would teach him even now how to develop that character. I ask that You would give both of us a purity of heart, mind, and body as we wait to meet and marry each other. I ask that You would make that day come quickly! I seek Your blessing on my future marriage. I ask that You would protect it and guard it so that a healthy heritage will begin through it.

This method doesn't limit your prayers to the day's focus, but it does serve as a reminder to intercede at least weekly for that which is important to you—it also gives you something to do when traffic is a little slower than you'd like!

Prayer Journal

Some people use a notebook, which offers the obvious convenience of transportability. I have an Excel spreadsheet on my laptop called "Things to Talk to Dad About." At the top is a list of column headings: *Date, For, Request, Date, Answered Prayer.* Now several pages long, this file documents all the ways God has answered my prayers over the years. When someone requests prayer, I add it to my spreadsheet. It serves as a reminder to follow through on my promise to pray for that person and also provides incentive to keep in touch to hear how it turns out. Since I don't have a commute on the weekend, I work through my list of not-yet-answered prayers on Saturdays and Sundays. When we take our concerns to God, we place them squarely in the hands of the One who can handle them.

While we speak to God primarily through prayer, He speaks to us primarily through His Word.

Study the Bible

When you check your mail each day, how do you prioritize your reading? On any given day, your stack might include a flyer announcing a grand opening, a coupon insert from a local business, a catalog from your favorite retailer, a stack of bills, postcard reminders to bring your dog to the vet and—Oh! a letter from a college friend! Which item do you choose to look at first? The letter, of course! With the popularity of e-mail and cell phones, receiving a handwritten letter is a rare event.

Letters are personal. They take time to write, and they relay the message that you are important to the sender. How many stacks of ribbon-tied letters are stored in the attics of America? Letters are precious.

The Bible is God's love letter to us. Though it has been misused to batter and abuse people over the course of history, that is certainly not God's intention. God allowed His Word to be written to reveal His thoughts, His ways, and His love. When we read it with a desire to understand His intent, His love for us becomes evident, and the truth about both Him and us becomes clear.

As I mentioned earlier, divorce can skew our understanding of the Bible. Throughout our life, our hurts have hindered our ability to see God and ourselves truthfully. Additionally, in the course of our daily lives the world's values bombard us. And more and more, the world's values are at odds with what God values. The truth is, God designed us and brought us into being. He knows the longings of our heart, and He weeps with us for our most hidden hurts. He has given us His Word as a guide for living our life in a way that will bring us all the joy and peace and contentment He longs for us to experience.

Elephants in India are chained to pegs when they are very young and weak. Day by day they grow bigger and stronger, until they could easily snap the pegs that hold them and escape their captivity. But they never realize this and docilely walk in circles, held back from freedom only by their illusions.[4]

We are often like the self-trapped elephant, held back by our own perceptions. We feel powerless when actually we have at our disposal tremendous energy. The realization that our chains can be broken is the first step toward snapping them.

God's Word has power, and equipped by it, we can break the chains of our own past. The book of Ephesians refers to God's Word as a sword, an offensive weapon used to ward off enemy attacks.[5] Many adult children of divorce wrestle with the following lies, but we can take these lies captive when we counter them with the truth contained in God's Word:

> **LIE:** I'm not worth much—even my parents abandoned me.
> **TRUTH:** I am of great worth because I was created in God's image! (See Genesis 1:27.)

> **LIE:** My life doesn't matter—I'm not a priority to anyone.
> **TRUTH:** God specifically created me with a unique purpose and plan! (See Jeremiah 29:11.)

> **LIE:** God doesn't care about me—after all, my parents were Christians and He didn't keep them from divorce—or me from the fallout.
> **TRUTH:** If God cares even about the sparrow, then how much more does He love me! (See Matthew 10:31.)

> **LIE:** Nothing good ever happens to me—even if something seems good, I can't believe that it will last.
> **TRUTH:** God promises to bring good out of even painful situations! (See Romans 8:28.)

LIE: I am a victim of my past—I will never get over the pain of my parents' divorce.

TRUTH: Though things seem rough now, God promises that my days of joy will return! (See Psalm 30:5.)

When we use the truth of God's Word to counter the lies we believe, we receive the power and privilege of our position as princes and princesses—children of the King! When God promises to provide for our needs, that includes filling in the gaps of our faulty thinking.

You'll find Scripture throughout this book that will speak to our needs as children of divorce, addressing our fears of abandonment and betrayal and our hopes for faithful love and a place to call home. When we know God's Word from memory, we can draw upon it for direction, instruction, and affirmation. I encourage you to commit especially personal passages to memory because you won't always have the ability or inclination to look them up in times of temptation.

Psalm 119:9,15 affirms that meditating on God's precepts and considering His ways will keep us pure. Doing so equips us to sift our life through the filter of our faith. As our mind becomes directed by the compass of conscience, our thoughts and feelings begin to submit to this truth.

As you study God's Word and grow in your faith, be intentional about applying and acquiring God's qualities, especially in areas where your tendency is not to do so. When you come upon an attribute of God, make a practical study of that trait in your journal. For example, for each characteristic list:

- *Trait:* What word describes God's character?
- *Scriptural reference:* Note the Bible verse.
- *Example:* Imagine a scenario where you can demonstrate this trait.

Here are a few to get you started:

- *God's involvement in my life is permanent* (see Deuteronomy

31:8). When I feel lonely, I will remind myself that I am not abandoned.

- *God is consistent* (see Hebrews 13:8). Household rules will be enforced because of their validity, not my mood. My love for my children will not be withdrawn based on their obedience or disobedience to those rules.
- *God is forgiving* (see 1 John 1:9). I will not define those around me by their past mistakes. I will do what I can to help each one become the person he or she is capable of being.

Take time occasionally to give yourself a spiritual checkup. Test your actual tendencies against the intentions of your list. For a more accurate evaluation, ask a friend or your spouse to share how well you convey the character you're aspiring to create. Remember that spiritual growth and healing take a lifetime. New experiences will illuminate additional tendencies and inclinations in need of healing and adjustment.

Journal

I prize my collection of nearly thirty notebooks and binders that chronicle my life. Each New Year's Day, I take out my journals from the past year to relive the blessings and learning experiences God has provided. Reading my reflections, I am encouraged by the evidence of my growing faith, as demonstrated by changes from how I initially viewed my circumstances, the things that concerned me, and the way I prayed.

My journals are filled with intercessory prayers for myself and others, my view of the events that affect me, verses that apply to the situations in my life and lie/truth contrasts like the previous examples. It gives me a sense of accomplishment and a glimpse of eternity to create such a tangible legacy for my children. My journals tell the story of a growing faith.

I first began journaling as the result of an assignment from my ninth-grade English teacher. I was sixteen, the first divorce was a decade decided, and the seeds of the second had already been sown. Reading those journal entries today, I see that the hurt I hid was displaced and displayed through some really depressing and death-fixated poetry! I lacked the self-awareness at the time to uncover the source of my dissatisfied state, so I struggled simply to make the feelings go away. By the time I was nineteen, I had learned to numb my feelings. It took nearly a decade to bring them back.

It is clear from my entries that I did not connect my struggles and the divorces until I picked up the book *Adult Children of Legal and Emotional Divorce* by Jim Conway. On September 2, 1993, I wrote:

> I can't believe that someone else feels the same way! Of course, after
> reading this book, it all makes so much sense. Of course divorce
> will bring a sense of loss and longing to my life. How have I missed
> it?! I'm reading it through a second time now, just a chapter before
> I go to bed so it'll sink in. My dreams have been really strange. I'm
> remembering a lot of events that I had blocked out. The author says
> that what I'm doing is reliving my childhood so that I can analyze
> my experiences as an adult. The glitch is that all those raw emotions
> are still there. I can't cry when I'm awake, but I've cried in my sleep.
> Lord, is this the way you're helping me grieve?

Many of my journal entries from my early twenties are written wrestling matches between my reality and what I wanted from my relationships—with God, my parents, my friends, my coworkers, and most especially with the men in my life. I was focused on what I wanted—a family, someone to care for me completely—and utterly unaware of how ill-equipped I was to contribute to a relationship. In October of 1993, I wrote:

> I've been studying what Your Word has to say about trust. I realize
> that my lack of trust (in anyone) isn't because I don't want to—and
> my friends haven't given me reason not to—I realize that I don't

know how to. There's some disconnect in my ability to believe that
I won't eventually be let down. Mom always told me to trust her
and she was the one who most betrayed my trust. Lord, Your Word
says to trust You with all my heart and to lean not on my own understanding (Proverbs 3:5-6). To lean on something is to put all my
weight against it because I know it will support me. I know I can
trust You. Is it really possible to lean on someone else without them
stepping away when they feel the pressure of my trust?

Reading a decade's worth of journals, I can see how I struggled to gain
a sense of stability even as I ran from every obstacle. If my job, a friend,
an environment—whatever—wasn't perfect, I looked for another. Because
I viewed my life as segmented by the divorces, I did not know how to create a sense of continuity in my life. Each break was a severe one. It wasn't
until I was in my late twenties that I made a conscious effort to connect
the dots of my life. In October of 2000, I wrote:

So I turned down the Chicago job. It's the first time I've turned
down a positive career move. I sense it's an outward sign of my
making an inward commitment to settle down. For the first time,
I'm looking at the whole of my life—not just the different areas of
my life, but the flow of it as well. Not everything in my life is good
right now. Some things are actually quite a challenge, but I feel
good about wanting to work through the hard stuff instead of
moving and starting all over again. I'm excited to dig in. I'm thankful for the friends and church family You have given me here. I
trust that they will walk through this valley with me.

I hope that as you read this book, your journal is capturing reflections
and insights that God may be nudging you to acknowledge. Journals
record the process of our progress.

One of the most effective ways of getting really honest about ourselves is to complete an exercise called the Retreat of Silence. A complete description is included in appendix B at the back of this book.

REFINER'S FIRE

One last point on this process of exchanging lies for truth:

> A group of women were studying the book of Malachi. As they were reading chapter three, they came across verse three, which says: "He will sit as a refiner and purifier of silver." This verse puzzled the women, and they wondered what this statement meant about the character and nature of God. One of the women offered to find out about the process of refining silver and get back to the group at their next Bible study.
>
> That week the woman called up a silversmith and made an appointment to watch him at work. She didn't mention anything about the reason for her interest in silver beyond her curiosity about the process of refinement. As she watched the silversmith, he held a piece of silver over the fire and let it heat up. He explained that in refining silver, one needed to hold the silver in the middle of the fire where the flames were hottest in order to burn away all the impurities. The woman thought about God holding us in such a hot spot—then she thought again about the verse, that He sits as a refiner and purifier of silver.
>
> She asked the silversmith if it were true that he had to sit there in front of the fire the whole time the silver was being refined. The man answered that yes, he not only had to sit there holding the silver, but he had to keep his eyes on the metal the entire time it was in the fire. If the silver was left even a moment too long in the flames, it would be destroyed.

The woman was silent for a moment. Then she asked the silversmith, "How do you know when the silver is fully refined?" He smiled at her and answered, "Oh, that's easy. It's finished when I can see my image in it."[6]

This process of burning off the impurities of our pasts is a painful one. We can take comfort in the fact that we are not alone in the heat, and that the Refiner of our heart will not let us be destroyed. Perhaps the hottest flames come from the challenges that arise when we try to show honor to parents whose actions and choices have not always been honorable to us.

Word

And without faith it is impossible to please God, because anyone who comes to him must believe that he exists and that he rewards those who earnestly seek him. (Hebrews 11:6)

Reflect

- What was the role of faith in your family?
- What is the role of faith in your life now?
- As you've studied the Bible, can you think of a way your family history influenced your understanding of the text?
- How has your relationship with your parents affected your understanding of God?
- What lies have you believed about the character of God, His love for you, and your worth? What truths should you believe?
- For a different perspective, ask your friends what lies they would say you believe.
- Consider the list of spiritual disciplines in this chapter. Which are you currently exercising? Based on what you read, do you feel a need or desire to adjust any of your spiritual habits?

Challenge

Take some time to write down the lies you wrestle with. For instance:

- *If I'm not the perfect Christian, God will be mad at me.*
- *If I am really nice and go the extra mile for people, others will like me.*

Then with the help of a godly mentor or Bible-study aids, combat these lies with the truth of Scripture. Write these truths on index cards and post them on your bathroom mirror or on the steering wheel of your car—anywhere you are likely to review them regularly. Ask God to help His truth seep into your soul and change your view of Him and how He feels about you.

Read

The Power of a Praying... series by Stormie Omartian (Harvest House)

The Lies We Believe by Chris Thurman (Nelson, 1991)

Growing Up Fatherless: Healing from the Absence of Dad by Mike Nappa (Baker, 2003)

The Ragamuffin Gospel by Brennan Manning (Multnomah, 2000)

Redefine Our Family Relationships

Effect: *The experience of divorce hinders our ability to form healthy relationships with our parents.*

Hope: *We can choose to adjust our expectations for our family relationships.*

Andrea was twenty when her parents divorced. While she never would have described her parents' marriage as a happy one, she took the fact that they were still married as evidence of their commitment to her family. At the time of the split, Andrea's dad moved in with his girlfriend, Sue, and announced his plans to marry her.

Andrea had enjoyed her newfound freedom during her first two years of college and was even a bit embarrassed by her parents' frequent calls and letters. After the divorce, when communication with her dad became less and less frequent, she began to struggle with depression.

Two years later, Sue was due to give birth the week of Andrea's graduation from college. Remembering the hours she and her dad had spent together poring over college brochures and researching schools online, Andrea never doubted that her dad would share the accomplishment of her big day.

A week before graduation, she called her father to arrange the details of his visit, mindful of the tension that still existed between her parents. Her father skirted the subject until Andrea finally asked him pointedly if he was coming. She relayed his response: "He told me that he was going to stay home because he needed to be at his child's birth. He was committed to making his new marriage work, and I needed to understand that Sue was his priority, not me. My parents both told me that their divorce wasn't about me. It sure feels to be about me now. Maybe if Dad would have put that kind of effort into his marriage with Mom, I wouldn't feel like the nothing I do now."

While our situations may not be exactly the same, the effect of divorce presents several collective concerns:

- We resent the inequity that causes us to tiptoe around our parents' preferences when their choices show us that we're not their priority.
- We feel cheated because our transition into adulthood is disrupted when roles are reversed and *we* are called upon to perform the "parental" duties of confidant, counselor, or buffer as we soften the blows of hurtful incoming messages.
- We are confused about what it means to honor our parents, particularly if they continue to mistreat us in the present. What, then, does it mean to honor them?

Am I Still a Priority to You?

Divorce rates skyrocketed at a time when popular psychology taught our parents that institutions such as church, family, and even marriage hindered their "true self." Happiness, however they chose to define it, was the ultimate goal, and to be healthy, they needed to pursue whatever might bring about that satisfaction, even divorce. Without an understanding of the ultimate fulfillment that comes through delayed gratification and the sacrifice of struggle, our parents divorced in droves, teaching us that marriage is disposable and families exist in flux.

Thirty-year-old Jason, whose parents divorced when he was three and who went on to endure multiple divorces on both sides in the years since, told me that his parents' divorces have hindered his ability to believe in the possibility of lifelong love. Though he very much hopes to be successful at marriage, he can't imagine another person making him a priority for a lifetime because his parents did not model that kind of commitment.

Divorce says to a child, "Your parents' quest for happiness is more important to them than your need for stability, their spouse's expectations for fidelity, and God's standard for integrity." Ironically, even if our parents' divorce is amicable because they are able to negotiate the details of their postdivorce life peacefully, we wonder if or why they couldn't have applied that same effort to preserve and improve their marriage.

Divorce often requires our parents to set aside their parenting role for a time (often a long one) as they regain their own security and stability. Unfortunately, this means they might be self-centered and oblivious to our needs as their children. Statistics tells us that more often than not, they don't take the time to find security and stability on their own but choose instead to look for it in the arms of a new lover, making the transition even more painful for us because we feel twice-abandoned. From our perspective, one parent has already left us, and now our remaining parent is telling us by their actions that they would rather spend time with someone other than us. This leads to a devastated sense of self-worth at a time in our life when our value needs to be established and/or affirmed.

WHY DO I FEEL LIKE THE PARENT?

Roles sometimes get reversed as our parents look to us for approval of their dates, significant others, and new spouses. It's as if our approval of their new life is the final step to their own closure.

When adultery is involved, it is extremely unfair of our parents to ask us to accept the person who had a part in our family's breakup. If we choose to accept Dad's new girlfriend, then we feel like we are sharing in

Mom's betrayal. If we decide to ignore Dad's new girlfriend, he may interpret it as a rejection of him.

In fact, the inner conflict intensifies if a parent asks us (or forces us) to participate in a remarriage ceremony shortly after the divorce. In addition to shattering any hopes that our parents may reconcile, our participation presumes an acceptance of the divorce that we may not have reached. And if this transition occurs when we are children, we are not developmentally able to articulate our unresolved sadness, especially in light of our parent's obvious happiness. We internalize our confusion until we reach a point of safe release, often not until adulthood.

Jill was a new mom when her parents divorced. At a time in her life when she wanted and needed her mom to affirm her and help her develop her own maternal skills, she was frustrated by her mom's giddy, detailed descriptions of her new dating adventures. Jill lamented, "Why do our parents get to be children just because we have grown up?"[1] In disgust, she turned more and more to her mother-in-law for counsel and resented the lost opportunity to share this season of life with her mom.

As a seventeen-year-old, Becky shares Jill's frustration. When her parents divorced, her mom dove into a deep depression. She came home each night and went directly to bed. As the oldest child, Becky felt responsible to care for her younger siblings and for the household chores. When her mom did interact with Becky, her words were filled with hopeless desperation. As Becky realized that her long-anticipated college tour was not going to happen over the summer, she vented in frustration, "You know, I need parents too!"

In the midst of the postdivorce adjustment, we may feel left to fend for ourselves. And when the emotional dust has settled, we may not want or know how to let our parents regain their roles as mom and dad. In the chaos of my family's postdivorce years, we separated to lick our wounds in our own private ways. By the time the issues of divorce surfaced in my adult relationships, I had already emotionally checked out of my family. A chasm in our collective history had to be bridged in order to build any common future. My dad, with whom I hadn't lived since I was six, had been remarried for several years and had a new family complete with four new children. John, my stepdad, with whom I lived from the first through the twelfth grades, had also remarried and was making a new life for himself. Only my mom was unmarried. I knew that I was related to all these people—physically and/or emotionally—but the family I grew up in—Mom, John, and I—no longer existed. The house I called home was no longer ours, and the place I longed to return to could only be found in the past. I wanted *one* home to return to, and I grieved for the home I no longer knew. I wanted to have a relationship with each of my parents, but I didn't know how to put the pieces together in a way that fit with the new life I had created for myself, in a way that nurtured the person I had become.

The Honor Dilemma

If we've had to take a "time-out" from our parents, at what point do we allow them access to our heart and life again? In other words, how do we reconcile the biblical mandate to honor our parents when, depending on the circumstances, a relationship with our parents may be counterproductive to our emotional health?

As one of the Ten Commandments, the Bible's directive to honor our parents can be wrongly used to beat us up emotionally when we're already beaten down. So what exactly is *honor?* Look up the word in a dictionary and you'll see that the term denotes admiration, respect, special courtesy, consideration, or esteem accorded to another as a right. Honor does not mean obey, submit, condone, or put yourself in harm's way.

Mary was highly motivated to determine how to honor her parents. At twenty-two, she left her highly dysfunctional family to marry a young seminary student. Now forty-four and a pastor's wife, Mary often counsels adult children of divorce on the issue of honor. Mary's parents divorced when she was six. Her father was an alcoholic and was diagnosed with bipolar disorder. Her mother ended up marrying and divorcing five more times. Even when her latest love interest didn't make it to the altar, he usually made himself at home. As a Christian, Mary felt motivated to show honor to them in some way.

While Mary could not find many honorable characteristics in her parents, she did make a conscious effort to keep from hating or criticizing them. She knew that neither her mom nor dad had a strong family background and that they lacked the skills to break the patterns of their own pasts. Her father had suffered abuse when he was a boy, and her mother was one of ten children who were often neglected by a mother overwhelmed with the burden of their care. Mary determined to speak kindly to her parents and graciously about them, even if she didn't interact with them frequently. Though they didn't share her faith, her parents tried to manipulate Mary's feelings by telling her that a "good Christian" would be more involved in her parents' lives. She prayed for understanding to know how to draw healthy, honoring boundaries. For the health of her own heart, she let go of her expectations about how her parents should treat her. When her dad died three years ago, Mary mourned the end of her opportunity to connect with him, but she was at peace because she had forgiven him long ago and had found ways to honor him despite his shortcomings and failures as a father.

Mary has learned how to honor her parents without putting herself in harm's way with them. My parents were not abusive, but understanding the complexity of our dynamics has been a struggle for years. Only recently have I gained some helpful insight.

PERMISSION TO REDEFINE OUR FAMILY RELATIONSHIPS

Even after I wrote my first draft of this chapter, my editor challenged me to rethink what we are biblically obligated to do. I was frustrated because

what I had written was not what I felt, but I didn't know how to syner-
gize what I thought I should do spiritually with what I felt able to do emotionally.

And then God stepped in. He inspired my pastor to share a study on
Jesus' relationship with His earthly family. It has changed my life, and
with his permission and prayers for your healing, I share it with you.

The Bible tells us precious little about Jesus' adult relationship with
His family, but what we do know is significant and applicable to our situation. Mark 3:20-21 tells us: "Then Jesus entered a house, and again a
crowd gathered, so that he and his disciples were not even able to eat.
When his family heard about this, they went to take charge of him, for
they said, 'He is out of his mind.' "

Our parents may not understand our need for distance and may
attribute motives to us that are not accurate. From Jesus' example, we can
take confidence that we are within our rights to avoid our families'
attempts to manipulate or control us. When our families do not enhance
our ability to live well, we are not obligated to spend time with them or
meet their expectations of us.

While we may need to distance ourselves from our families, God
does not grant us permission to be vengeful in the interim. As the oldest
son in Jewish culture, Jesus was responsible for his widowed mom's welfare. Even though His family earlier had thought He was crazy, and
despite the fact that He was hanging on the cross in agonizing humilia-
tion, Jesus was willing to provide for His mom's needs by asking John to
take care of her.

John 19:25-27 illustrates:

Near the cross of Jesus stood his mother, his mother's sister,
Mary the wife of Clopas, and Mary Magdalene. When Jesus
saw his mother there, and the disciple whom he loved standing
nearby, he said to his mother, "Dear woman, here is your son,"

and to the disciple, "Here is your mother." From that time on, this disciple took her into his home.

Jesus didn't use the hurts His family caused as justification to be bitter against them. As children of divorce, we may not be able to have close relationships with our parents, but we can still look for ways to minister to them and provide for them—not just materially, but emotionally and spiritually as well. Depending on the relationship, however, we may need to limit our interactions to indirect contact, such as letters, e-mails, and prayers.

We do not honor our parents by pretending things are as we wish they were; we do it by opening ourselves to being used by God in a positive way in our parents' lives. A good test to gauge the tenderness of your heart is to ask yourself: If God were to change my parents so that they became what I've needed them to be, would I be willing to accept those changes, or would my bitterness prevent me from believing that they *could* change?

God provides us with the privilege of sharing with others—even our parents—the grace we've embraced. We can choose to do what is right, even when the object of our action doesn't reciprocate. In doing so, we are pleasing the Father we ultimately want to honor. Regardless of how our parents have treated or are treating us, we can take steps toward healing. We can redefine our relationships with them so that we honor them while protecting ourselves from further harm.

CREATE A DIFFERENT WAY OF RELATING

Each divorced family has its own dysfunctions. With that acknowledgment, we can personalize the following suggestions to create a different way of relating to our parents.

Establish Healthy Boundaries

In their landmark book *Boundaries,* Drs. Henry Cloud and John Townsend define boundaries as "a personal property line that marks those
things for which we are responsible. In other words, boundaries define
who we are and who we are not."[2]

As adults, we have the right to decide how much time we are going
to spend with our parents and how that time will be spent. While our parents may attempt to manipulate us with guilt or shame, we can rest
assured that establishing clear boundaries is a sign of emotional health. To
help you get started in delineating your own personal boundaries, consider the following examples.

I Will Limit My Parents' Influence on My Life

Sometimes it's just not in our best interest to spend time with our family
members. They may be abusive, abrasive, or otherwise a hindrance to our
emotional health. If so, it may be appropriate to create some distance as
we create new patterns of relating and interacting with them.

When it comes to his family of origin, twenty-four-year-old Simon
says his relationships feel forced. For example, his father, who rarely had
time for him after the divorce, is now physically challenged and pressures
for frequent visits. But for Simon, anything more than twice a month—
his childhood visitation schedule—is uncomfortable, so he limits his visits
to that.

Hannah, whose parents divorced when she was two, spent years frustrated by awkward arrangements that required her to spend time with a
father she didn't know. As she got older, the visits became counterproductive to her natural desire to spend more time with friends. She compared
her weekends with her dad to a prison sentence: "He did the crime and I
have to pay." Even after she moved out of state after college graduation,
her father made her feel guilty unless she spent her annual vacation with

him, even though she would have rather used those precious few days in other ways. At twenty-five, she demanded her right to stop the visits to a man she hardly knew by saying, "I've done my time and now I need to be free." Once Hannah articulated this boundary to her dad, she celebrated by using her single week of vacation on a trip that *she* wanted to take, free from the burden of an obligatory visit.

If, like Hannah, you dread long visits and the hassle of trying to hit all your homes, you have a right to use vacation time on a trip you can look forward to. If you don't trust your parents' ability to give you wise counsel, you have the right to find your own mentors and models. It's important to remember that there is nothing wrong or "bad" about you if you decide to limit your parents' interaction and influence with you.

I Will Not Allow My Parents to Guilt-Trip or Shame Me into Choosing Sides

Divorce had a devastating effect on our parents' egos. Especially if their identities were primarily drawn from their roles as spouses, they may feel an intense need to know that they have not lost us as well. Whether out of anger or in an attempt to assure themselves or justify their behavior, they may smother us with details we do not need to know.

Chad's parents divorced the Christmas after he started college. He left home that fall assuming everything was fine at home and that he had a home to return to. During the holiday break, Chad was stunned to learn not only that his parents were divorcing but that his perception of his family was faulty. As each parent pulled Chad aside to share his or her side of the story, it became clear that his parents were more interested in asserting their own innocence in an effort to gain Chad's support than they were in acknowledging that they each played a part in their divorce. Chad's impression of his parents instantly changed from stable advisors to selfish manipulators.

It is not appropriate for our parents to vent to us about each other or to try to recruit us to be on "their side." While they may think that talking about personal things keeps us included and informed, we can keep our boundaries intact by encouraging them to find a support group, friend, pastor, or counselor with whom they can discuss inappropriate feelings and situations.

I Will Not Be a Counselor to My Parents

Divorce often fast-forwards our relationships from that of parent and child to that of perceived peers. Especially during our older teen or young adult years, our parents can fall into the temptation of leaning on us for their emotional support instead of supporting us through our own trauma.

While it is natural and healthy for children to take care of their parents in their twilight years, it is not okay for our parents to supersede our emotional needs and development. We cannot enable our parents to become dependent on us as their counselors, messengers, roommates, or confidants if doing so denies us the freedom to state and show love for both parents equally. We need to let Mom and Dad remain our parents, even though their parenting skills may be (or may have been) lacking.

A good test to tell if our parents are violating this boundary is to ask ourselves if they would share this same information with us—or seek this information from us—if they were happily married.

Focus on the Feasible

There are certain things we simply cannot control. We cannot control our parents' willingness (or unwillingness) to make choices that respect us. We cannot control how they might interpret our need to process our pain. We cannot control how they might respond to our need for new boundaries that protect our healing hearts. However, we can focus on the feasible, on what we can control.

After her parents divorced, Jodi, a textbook people pleaser, bent over backward to avoid any situation that might make her parents feel uncomfortable. She dutifully planned two Christmases, two birthdays, even two celebrations of her college graduation so that her parents wouldn't have to interact with each other. When she got engaged at age twenty-eight, she began planning two weddings until her fiancé issued an ultimatum: "It doesn't make sense to spend all that extra money on two weddings. Your parents have been divorced for ten years. If they want to participate in our day, they can choose to do so without jeopardizing our financial future."

Matt experienced a similar turning point when his first child was born. He reflected, "I've come to the conclusion that the times we get hurt the most are when we put expectations on the way people 'should' act. They never seem to meet those expectations. I think that we can't 'get over' our hurt until we quit putting those expectations on other people."

Before the big day Matt sent a strongly worded e-mail to both his parents, telling them they would each get a call when his wife went into labor. They needed to know that the other might be at the hospital. If they decided they weren't comfortable with that arrangement, they could stay home and live with the fact that they allowed their own selfishness to cause them to miss their grandchild's birth. Matt realized he was not responsible for his parents' feelings or choices. Instead, he focused on what he could control. In this case, Matt chose to make a priority of caring for his wife and giving his attention to the arrival of his child.

Guard Against Resentment

Even though we may have forgiven our parents for the hurts they inflicted on us in the past, we must continually guard against resurrecting our resentments—or becoming bitter over new ones. In addition to the principles presented in chapter 2, we can keep our heart tender toward our parents, even if we don't interact with them, by:

- praying for their best interest
- choosing not to dwell on negative thoughts
- refusing to relive resentful moments

- allowing someone we trust to hold us accountable to being open to a restored relationship with our family

Accept the Family Structure As It Is

At some point in our healing, we must reconcile the difference between what our families are and what we think they should be. We've likely come to terms with the fact that Mom and Dad will never share a home together again. However, we must also accept the possibility that our parents may not regain the ability to be "Mom" and "Dad" to us in the way that we wish they could.

As I was growing up, my custody arrangement gave me an everyday dad and a special-occasion dad. My stepfather lived with me, and I saw my biological dad a couple of times a month and on special occasions. After Mom and John divorced—and John wasn't able to be my everyday dad anymore—I spent over a decade expecting my biological dad to fill that role. This resulted in a perpetual state of frustration for me because desire alone could not rebuild the twenty-five years we spent apart. It took an awkward vacation together for me to realize that I will never have the kind of intimate relationship with my dad that my stepsisters and half-sisters enjoy. I had to let go of that expectation and allow God to be my only everyday Dad.

For twenty-four-year-old Simon, acceptance came with the realization that he had subconsciously re-created his visitation schedule as an adult. After his parents divorced when he was three, they followed the traditional schedule of every-other-weekend visits. Though Simon knew his dad and had many shared experiences with him, his father never, as Simon described, "had his heart." He continued, "My stepdad was my real dad. I hate it when people assume that my bio dad is my real dad. My father is just this guy that I spent time with a couple times a month. I remember in college listening to a friend talk about a favorite uncle. That's how I felt about my dad. Now I refer to my father as Uncle Dad."

Seek the Good in Our Parents

John Trent is a counselor, author, and child of divorce. In his book *Pictures the Heart Remembers,* John tells the story of how he, as a young boy, found a newspaper clipping with a picture of a man in military dress. His mom explained that the man in the picture was his father, and the article explained that he won a medal for his bravery in battle. Despite the fact that his father abandoned the family when John was two months old, John was smitten with the idea that his daddy was a hero. He held his father in high esteem—with only a photo to build a relationship on—until, as a teen, John lingered on a high-school football field long after the lights had dimmed, waiting to meet a father who never came.

Most people would accept John's justification for dismissing his dad. Yet, he wrote,

It's not very big, particularly considering how much it represents. It's just a medium-sized shadowbox frame containing my father's faded army cap, two rows of campaign ribbons, a purple heart with clusters for being wounded three different times, and a bronze star.

The frame is hung purposely in a very special place in our home, right above the family piano. Why there? Because our precious younger daughter, Laura, is an aspiring pianist. She's following in her cherished older sister Kari's steps, dutifully practicing day after day. When the girls sit at our small upright piano, struggling through scales and sonatas, they can look up at that frame and be reminded of their grandfather. It's there because I believe the words of Ralph Waldo Emerson: "Every man is entitled to be valued by his best moment."

Truthfully, there weren't many "best moments" in my relationship with my father.... But there's that shadowbox. It hangs above the piano because it's a picture of a time when my father displayed love of country and courage under fire. It is a visual reminder that he endured his own share of horror. His heroism is captured in his ribbons and medals and that old faded hat. They're a "best moment" for the girls to look up at and remember their grandfather at his most noble.[3]

Our parents followed their hearts and had every intention of making their marriages work. They did some good things—do you remember?—and made some bad decisions. They did the very best they could with the knowledge and skills they had at the time they made those tough decisions. And just like all of us, they are dealing—every day—with the consequences of their choices.

AN ACT OF FAITH

We don't always know why God allows us to experience the things He does, including being born to parents who would divorce. But we can be confident that He has a plan. Romans 8:28 promises that "in all things God works for the good of those who love him, who have been called according to his purpose." It doesn't say that all things that happen to us are good, or that if we love God we will always get what we want. But it does promise that if we love God and seek His will and perspective, then whatever happens to us will be worked for good.

As children of divorce, we have a choice. We can choose to see ourselves as victims of our circumstances and react accordingly, surrendering our power to change direction. Or we can choose to see ourselves as God's children and invite Him to fill us with the peace, joy, and love we yearn for.

Divorce isn't anyone's first choice. But regardless of our earthly parents' decisions, our heavenly Father desires that we match hurt not with more hurt, but with healing. At times, the most honorable thing is to act in faith, choosing to respond in a loving way to those who have hurt us, trusting God to let the feelings follow. It is not fair to pigeonhole our parents because of their past choices. Instead, we can give them the freedom to be who they are today, free from the lens of their pasts and free to grow and learn from their divorce. Look for opportunities to connect with your parents. Decide to seek the good in them. Embrace the grace that God has given you and extend it to your parents.

Word

> If it is possible, as far as it depends on you, live at peace with everyone. (Romans 12:18)

Reflect

- How has divorced affected your sense and understanding of family?
- How would you describe the current relationship you have with your parents? What roles do they play in your life?
- How would you describe the ideal relationship with your parents at this stage in your life? What roles would they play? Think about older couples you admire for ideas.
- What boundaries do you need to establish with your parents? How will you make sure they are respected?
- What does "honor your parents" look like for you?
- What five positive traditions or traits modeled by your parents do you want to continue with your own family?
- What five tendencies or habits modeled by your parents do you want to change with your own family? How will you do things differently?

- Consider how you want your kids (should you have any) to describe you. What kind of parent do you want to be when they are under age five? in middle school? in high school? in college? adults? parents? Think of a couple at each of these stages who can serve as a model for you.

Challenge

Write a tribute letter to each of your parents. Acknowledge the good things they have done and share the positive lessons they have taught you.

Read

    A Father's Legacy (J. Countryman, 2000)
    Boundaries by Dr. Henry Cloud and Dr. John Townsend
       (Zondervan, 1992)
    Pictures the Heart Remembers by John Trent (WaterBrook, 2000)
    Reflections of a Mother's Heart (J. Countryman, 2000)

Find Home for Ourselves

Effect: *The experience of divorce robs us of a secure sense of belonging.*

Hope: *We can choose to adopt a new definition of family.*

The classic drama *Kramer vs. Kramer* hit theaters in 1979, the same year my mom and dad divorced. The film presents a microcosm of American culture as Joanna Kramer (Meryl Streep), an unfulfilled homemaker, leaves her husband, Ted (Dustin Hoffman), and six-year-old son, Billy (Justin Henry), to "find herself." During her absence, Ted learns to connect with his son and balance his work and home lives. Eighteen months later, Joanna returns to reclaim her son. In the ensuing custody battle, the issues of divorce and self-actualization, women's rights and parental involvement are all entwined and defined according to the self-affirming wisdom of the late '70s.

In the final scene, Joanna comes to pick up Billy, of whom she has been awarded custody. But first, she meets Ted in the lobby. We see Joanna emotionally break down as she describes her regret that she didn't paint familiar clouds on Billy's new bedroom walls. Familiar wall décor cannot replace the familiarity of family as it was, and as she speaks, Joanna realizes that although she came to take her son home, he already *is* home. She steps into the elevator to tell Billy that he can stay with his dad. As the doors close and the credits play, we are left to imagine that this newly fragmented family has reached an acceptable closure.

I recently watched the movie again for the first time as an adult. The poignancy was still palpable as I was transported to a memory, a distant time when Dad and Mom lived under one roof. When the elevator doors closed this time, I wondered what the sequel would say twenty-some years later, from Billy's perspective. Would he think he was home simply because he had the same cloud-painted bedroom in each parent's home? Did he feel equally comfortable in both of the homes his parents undoubtedly took great care to create for him, or did he feel equally unsettled in both? Did Ted or Joanna remarry? If so, did they have additional children? If so, how did those siblings affect Billy's sense of home? Did the attention his parents lavished on their "new" children with their "new" spouses make Billy feel displaced? How did Billy deal with the discomfort of knowing that he was the tangible reminder of his parents' failed marriage? When Billy graduated and moved out on his own, to which home did he return on his limited vacations? When he married, how did he and his bride decide where to spend the holidays? When his first child was born, was he able to share that event with both sets of parents?

Losing Home

At the time of our parents' divorce, we could see the physical breakup of our homes, and while we acutely felt the pain of our parents' partings, we couldn't know then how much more we would miss as we grew to understand all that home was meant to be.

Much of the writing of this book coincided with MTV's 2001 *Real World* season, where, ironically, all seven participants were children of divorce. Before the season began, MTV aired a casting special to give a glimpse into the selection process. In an introductory segment, one potential cast member spoke for a generation when she said, "People ask me where home is, and I'm torn. Home is where the heart is, and my heart is torn."[1]

As I've pointed out, our experiences of divorce follow different trajectories than those of our parents. We all begin in a comfortable place: our parents in love and we in one home. While our parents spent an intense period of turmoil before making the decision to divorce, we often had no clue that our homes were about to break. Even when battles raged down the hall, we didn't believe our parents would divorce. Our parents' pain peaked in the period of parting. In the immediate aftermath they threw themselves into adjustment, and we adapted to what was thrust upon us.

As children, we could not articulate how our parents' process of symbolizing their own fresh start was often exactly that which undermined our own stability. The act of "de-mom-ifying" or "de-dad-ifying" took away from us the very things we most yearned to cherish, the artifacts of our history. When photographs, videos, clothes, houses, and other mementos of home as we knew it were disassembled, boxed up, thrown away, or sold, we couldn't help but be unsettled by the change.

Until recently others have assumed that we, too, experience our most profound suffering at the time of divorce. No question, that was an intensely difficult transition for us all. And yet, after the divorce, our parents felt a sense of relief or at least hope that their situations *could* get better. A difficult chapter was closed, and they were free to move on and even marry again. But as children, we couldn't draw the lines so clearly. The past was all we knew, and we had no means to predict the future.

In the years following the divorce while we were still living under our parents' roofs, we—like all adolescents—looked ahead to our emancipation. We hoped the tension of balancing two lives would lessen when we were no longer encumbered by custody arrangements and two sets of household rules. In reality, the divorce follows us wherever we go. Our crisis crescendoes as we realize that *we* are now responsible for deciding where home is, and often we discover that we're not sure of the answer.

This is the crux of the sleeper effect: The full impact of divorce does not manifest itself until we are on our own, finding home, and seeking our own romantic relationships. Elizabeth Marquardt explained her own research on the sleeper effect this way:

> In my interviews I observed that many young people first begin
> to experience palpable grief and anger about their parents' divorce
> when they go to college. Living at college is the first time they have
> some physical and emotional distance from the post-divorce family
> and thus it is their first opportunity to reflect on it. Further, visita-
> tion patterns that had been established earlier must be re-negoti-
> ated now that the young person only goes home for summer and
> holiday breaks, and this brings up painful questions of commit-
> ment to their parents and competition between them. In addition,
> the close relationships they form in college give them opportunities
> to observe their peers' experiences in intact families, and they begin
> to wonder what it would have been like to grow up that way.[2]

Of all the topics discussed in my surveys and interviews with repre-
sentatives of Generation Ex, the request to define "home" elicited the
most emphatic response. The replies reflected a mix of loss and longing.
They often defined "home" as an experience denied: a safe place, a sanctuary, a peaceful place where we are unconditionally loved. Ryan wrote "a
roof over my head, a place to sleep...a place I must provide for myself."
Twenty-two-year-old Bill stated, "Home is where I lick my wounds." For
us, however, home is more likely to be the place where our most serious
emotional wounds were inflicted.

Many referred to home in either the past tense or as a future hope.
While home is a place to our friends, it is often a memory to us. One
woman looking at home in the rear view mirror replied, "I've been told
that home is where your heart is...but then I can never go home because
now it's someone else's house. My happy memories are still trapped there."

Home is a frequent daydream, a desire to dwell upon. Michael captured the longing by writing, "Home is more than a permanent address, it is permanence." Nineteen-year-old Amber reflected, "Home is a place where good memories are formed, where you stay for a while and it grows old with you, where those traditions never change. Home is a place that on this Earth I have not yet had." Twenty-seven-year-old Allyson simply said, "Home is a place where love exists." Our revised history might say, "Home is a place where love existed." For many children of divorce, thoughts of home lead to thoughts of loss rather than love. Home is a collection of dusty photographs and neglected memories.

Even those who were adults when their parents said, "I don't," described the loss of home as profound: "I don't know why I feel so terrible," Amy explained. "I am a grown woman with kids of my own. But now it feels that one part of my life—my childhood that I long ago left behind—is now gone forever. I no longer have a 'home' to go to."

John noted our loss this way, "Even if you don't live there, home is supposed to be your safety net, and now there is no such thing as home anymore." Shannon reflected on one of the most jarring adjustments for those who were adults when their parents divorced. She said, "During my whole childhood they were the *only* parents of all my friends still together. They always held hands and cuddled. Our home was one full of laughter and happy times. I always said when I get married I want to be like them... Look at them now." When our "good" home breaks, we feel that what we had known was a lie, and we struggle to sift out what is still true.

As a concession, we might look to our grandparents to provide a symbol of home. Megan wrote, "I found that after leaving home, my grandparents' home became the place where I felt stability and love. I know their house as my home." In my own experience, Gramma and Grampa Hemza, married sixty-plus years, remained in my old neighborhood long after my parents and I had moved out. Home for me was a return to their house. With their deaths, I felt a finality to my displacement.

Our parents may have worked hard to give us a sense of home in both of their dwellings—two rooms of our own, two sets of toys and clothes and things. And yet, we still felt unsettled because although we were members of two households, we didn't share in the complete history of either. We simply could not be in two places at once, so no matter where we were, we were missing out on something at our other home. We could not create a comfortable familiarity with someone we saw only every other weekend and on special occasions. Home is the comfort of one shared last name under one shared roof. Home is not made from the extraordinary, but from the ordinary. Home is made of countless seemingly meaningless moments of monotony: Sunday mornings reading the paper (comics first), Saturday morning chores (bathrooms last), endless patterns and traditions undefined until they disappear.

As young adults, we face a dilemma with each vacation: Which "home" do we go home to? If we stay with one but not the other, we feel guilty. If one parent is remarried and the other is not, how can we spend time with the married parent with the other feeling betrayed? As family structure changes, how do we know which role we are expected to play? If we were the cute, youngest child with Mom and Dad, how do we adjust to being the big sister to a much younger sibling we don't even know? If Mom remarries when we are an adult, what kind of relationship are we supposed to have with our new stepdad? Or with his kids?

Like twenty-three-year-old Scott, we may issue an ultimatum to our parents: "I've moved around and catered to your choices all my life, missing out on trips and vacations so I could spend equal time with both of you. I'm an adult now, so it's your turn to cater to me. If you want to see me, you can come to my place. I'm not going to live my life in response to your choice anymore."

Marriage sometimes adds to our sense of instability. Julie, whose husband is also an adult child of divorce, reflected, "You are always dealing with blended-family issues, and there is never a sense of complete comfort and familiarity. My husband feels just as uncomfortable going to his dad's as I do because he doesn't know his stepmother that well."

In frustration, we may avoid the decision of where to go altogether, and instead spend holidays with a friend's intact family. And in doing so, we become more acutely aware of what we have missed.

For me, intact families have become a sort of holy grail. I gravitate toward friends whose parents are still married. But even when invited to participate in their family festivities, I still feel out of place, as if they all have a part in a play I haven't read and I'm just a member of the audience inappropriately crashing the stage. When it comes to families, I can't seem to escape the feeling of being an outsider.

Caught between the memory of home and the hope of a future home, we wrestle to define what home means to us in the present. While we cannot change the past, we can change our response to it. We can find home when we give ourselves permission to grieve our loss and initiate a new definition of home.

GRIEVING OUR LOSS OF HOME

In chapter 2 we talked about our need to grieve the hurt we feel as a result of our parents' divorce, and that grief is not a one-time experience. Our life and family will never again be as God intended. It's not fair. It's not best. But it is our reality. This reality is a loss to grieve, as many times as necessary. Facing our pain lessens its power over us. It is now a known enemy, and though it may continue to confront us, we no longer have to be surprised by its attacks.

If our parents divorced when we were young, we need to mourn our loss of childhood and the order and stability that defines an intact family. The divorce disrupted our transition to adulthood and may have required us to grow up too quickly. As adults, a part of us is still trapped as that little boy or little girl hungry for Mommy or Daddy. As one woman reflected, "Sometimes I want to turn back time and become the little girl that used to crawl onto Daddy's lap and know that he'd make everything okay." The problem is that we are no longer little boys and little girls and Daddy no longer holds the power to solve our problems.

I was thirty and in my first serious relationship before I recognized my own need to grieve the loss of my childhood. As I met with a counselor to affirm my emotional readiness for marriage, I realized that the driving force behind my desire to marry into a nuclear Christian family was to reprise my role as the little girl. I wanted to marry into the kind of family in which my father-in-law would play the "father" role I had idealized. My counselor challenged me with this truth: I could still have that kind of family, but I would have to be in the role of "mom," not "daughter." I tried to defend my dream by asserting my hope for a tangible model of committed Christian love, but I couldn't deny the reality of my now-named loss.

In addition to grieving the loss of the home of our hope, we may also need to mourn the loss of family traditions. Before Erin's parents divorced when she was fourteen, they made a big deal out of birthdays. She remembers, "On the morning of each birthday, Dad would deliver our favorite breakfast to us in bed. Mom would make special treats for me to share at school, and in the afternoon my friends would come over for a specially themed party. There was the Cabbage Patch party, the E.T. party... Each year was better than the last. Until the divorce. They split two months before my birthday. That year, Mom didn't even remember until I reminded her, and Dad forgot completely. I haven't really wanted to celebrate my birthday since."

One of the most original grieving rituals I've discovered involved a funeral that one adult child of divorce held for her family. She describes the service in great detail on her Web site, beginning with the formal invitation:

You are cordially invited
to read about the funeral

of my family
held in honor of twenty-five years
of family togetherness.

For the service, Sue gathered family mementos, including the topper from her parents' wedding cake and a family picture, and placed them in a tin. She added a personal note and placed it in the tin as well. On a day that was significant to her, she found a spot in her backyard, buried the container, and performed a ceremony. The ritual was complete with music—"The Lord's Prayer" (Aaron Neville), "Until I Fall Away" (Gin Blossoms), the "Funeral March" (Frederic Chopin), and "Sorry Seems to Be the Hardest Word" (Elton John). As she conducted her ceremony, she prayed and remembered and grieved. When she was finished, she filled in the hole and placed flowers from her dad on the dirt.

On her site, she wrote, "I felt a sense of closure. Something concrete was done to symbolize the end for my family. I was glad I was alone and I was glad to have picked such poignant music. I would recommend this for anyone who is still in a lot of pain, like I am, and I know a lot of us are. It really helped and it was something active; it made me feel less like a victim of this whole thing."[3]

We need to mourn the abrupt end to our childhood innocence and allow our family of origin to be who they are now. They may not be Mommy or Daddy, but maybe they can be Mom and Dad. When we have grieved what we lost or will never have—and all that this means to us—we can create a home in the present. We can realize that home begins with where we are and to whom we belong.

REDEFINING HOME

When we let go of our expectation of home from our families of origin, we are free to redefine home and seek relationships with people who can provide the safety and nurture all of us need. For married children of divorce, a sense of home naturally develops with our spouses and children. Though the process is not without its trials, as we leave and cleave to our spouses, we create new families and homes of our own.

For singles, redefining home can be more challenging, yet it is possible. Here are some suggestions I have found helpful.

Accumulate a Family of Friends

We can find home in a family of friends with whom we create covenant relationships. With an intentional commitment, these friends can stand in for parents and family who might be unwilling or unable to provide us with consistent, unconditional support.

We can gain a sense of family with our friends by creating with them the habits of healthy interactions. For example, a group of singles can feel like family when they sit together at church, spend holidays together, and create their own traditions together.

While we are not able to choose our families of origin, we can create our own families of choice. Simon describes his family of choice as those who "have his heart." When his engagement was called off because his mom's many marriages caused his future in-laws to cast doubt on his own ability to commit, the people who had his heart were the ones he trusted to comfort him in his grief.

We accumulate a family of friends by inviting others who demonstrate the characteristics we want to emulate into relationships of intentional interdependence.

By God's grace, I was able to create my own family of choice in the spring of 2000. Six months after moving to Michigan, I was experiencing a real hunger for intimate friendships. My friends were scattered around the country like markers of my many moves. I didn't have anyone with whom I could share the day-to-day details of my life. In a step of faith, I decided to attend a weekend retreat. When we broke into small groups

that first night, we were asked to share our deepest need. I disclosed that
I had been praying for three or four women to become my "family of
friends."

My need resonated with one of the women in my group. That evening,
we found two other women who shared a similar experience in their group.
The next day, the four of us went on a long, bonding walk and talked about
our mutual need for intimate connection and accountability. On that walk,
we all agreed to enter into a covenant friendship with one another. With
that intentional act, we forfeited our right to simply walk away when disagreements surfaced. As a family of friends, we are committed to working
things out with one another. And in doing so, we are demonstrating the
depth of commitment necessary for a successful relationship, particularly a
lifelong marriage. With the addition of another godly woman a short while
later, I have found home for myself in the creation of my family of choice.
(I talk more about my relationship with these women in chapter 7.)

Accountability to others may be something new to you, especially
because we live in a culture that values independence over interdependence. But lifelong love and commitment are rooted in the truth that we
need others. As we learn to be authentic and vulnerable with those we
choose as our family of friends, we form a pattern of healthy attachment
that we can then bring into our marriages and pass down to our children
and future generations.

Accept Our Adoption into a Spiritual Family

Our longing for home is rooted in a yearning for stability, structure, and
sentiments that don't change. As children of divorce, we may not be able
to find these things in the people we call Mom and Dad, but we can claim
them in our identity as children of God. When holidays and special events
disorient us, we can claim the promise of Psalm 90:1: "Lord, through all
the generations you have been our home!" (NLT).

The adoption optioned to us through Christ is a fitting analogy to both our physical and spiritual condition. There is a parallel between our longing for the home that was and the home that will be. When we begin to see ourselves first and foremost as God's son or daughter, we find the stability of a Father who is unchanging, the structure of a family in which our place is permanent, and the safety of a love that is unconditional.

In 1999, contemporary Christian artist Steven Curtis Chapman beautifully illustrated this analogy in a song he wrote for his adopted daughter, Shaohannah. "When Love Takes You In" holds double meaning as the lyrics express the longing for home and belonging the orphan baby and we, as humans, experience. When I interviewed Steven for Family Christian.com, he explained the meaning behind the lyrics by saying,

> Just as soon as that drop of rain hits the sea, it will never be a drop
> of rain again. Now it's become a part of something so much bigger.
> I thought, "That's what happens for us in Christ." [God] says, "I
> won't leave you as orphans. I've come for you." Love has come and
> taken us in.... The wildest dream would be that love would take
> me in and that I would have a home and I would actually be a
> part of a family. And yet that's what happened [for Shaohannah
> when we adopted her, and for all of us as we become part of the
> family of God].[4]

Steven knows the loss of home. He penned the perennial wedding classic, "I Will Be Here," as affirmation of fidelity to his young bride in light of the breakup of his parents' thirty-year marriage shortly after his own wedding day.

Assimilate into a Church Family

If we consider our adopted place in God's family, we'll realize that we have millions of brothers and sisters with whom we share our inheritance. These men and women will be our family for eternity. The context estab-

lished for us to learn to get along together is the local church. Getting involved in a church is a way to set down our own roots and find a sense of belonging with others who are like-minded.

As someone who has moved a lot, I know how difficult it can be to find a new church home—or to even be motivated to find one, for that matter. We've dealt with enough abandonment in our life. We may not be up for risking rejection from a place that is supposed to accept us. It can be frustrating finding a place where we feel comfortable, yet challenged to grow. A word of warning: Don't look for the perfect church. It doesn't exist. The church is made up of imperfect people loved by a perfect God.

Here are a few tips for finding a church home.

- *Ask around.* Where do your friends and colleagues go?
- *Know what you're looking for.* Do you want contemporary or traditional worship? What style of teaching do you prefer? What activities and ministries are important to you?
- *Check your attitude.* Ask, "Which church needs what I have to offer?" not "What can I get from this church?"
- *Get a copy of the doctrinal statement and check it against the Bible.* A good church will have Bible references for their beliefs.
- *Don't be too quick to judge.* The pastor may be out of town or having a bad day. Easter Sunday will not show a typical crowd; neither will Super Bowl Sunday. Visit a church two or three times before making a decision.
- *Set a deadline to make a decision.* American Christians in particular have adopted a window-shopping mentality: always looking, never buying. That approach may work for your budget, but it will hinder your spiritual growth.
- *As with any major decision, pray.* Ask God to guide you to a body with challenging teaching, engaging worship, committed members, and a need that only you can meet. Then join that body and meet that need!

Within the context of the church, seek out a married couple old enough to be your parents and spiritually mature enough to provide a living example of how you would like to live your life in the future. Especially if your own parents aren't Christian or live far away, you can benefit from the wisdom of another couple who can provide "parental" advice. As you develop a relationship with them, be intentional about sharing why you are developing an intimacy with them and how you would like to see them engage in your life.

Though the percentage of people who share our background is continuing to grow, many churches don't know how to meet our needs. As we choose to engage with our church families, we can create an environment where our need for home is met. Families in the church can reach out to adopt those of us without families of our own. No one in the church should have to spend a holiday alone. The onus is not only on others to reach out to us; we have been empowered to serve as well. The best way to feel involved is to get involved. As we become more focused on meeting the needs of others, we will be less hindered by our own hurts and more ready to achieve the health that defines a person who is whole.

Word

Lord, through all the generations you have been our home!
(Psalm 90:1, NLT)

Reflect

- What does "home" mean to you?
- How have holiday celebrations changed since your parents divorced? How does this arrangement make you feel?
- In what way do you feel part of a family of choice? of God's family?
- In what way does your experience relate to that of an adoptee? someone whose parent has died?

- When you think of *home,* does the word most vividly conjure up feelings that are past-, present-, or future-oriented? In what way?
- Have you believed that a family of your own would bring you closure? If you are married, have you found that to be true? If you are single, have you found yourself distracted by this desire?
- How has a lack of continuous shared history affected your intimacy with family members?

Challenge

Find at least one couple, family, or friend who would be willing to fulfill a family-type role in your life.

Read

Being the Body by Charles Colson (W Publishing, 2003)

Finding a Mentor, Being a Mentor by Donna Otto (Harvest House, 2001)

6

Seek Wholeness

Effect: The experience of divorce leaves us with a linger-
           ing sense of being broken or incomplete.

Hope: We can choose to be healthy and whole.

May 21, 1978

Dear Jenny,

Last night when we were saying prayers, you made a comment that
made my heart sad. You said that all the mothers up where your
mom is living stay home at night and that your mother is the only
one in the whole world that doesn't. It struck me that each child
whose parents are having marriage problems at some point realizes
that her parents aren't like other parents. It hurts me to think that
soon you may be realizing that people will be saying you are from
a broken home and how that might change your self-concept and
confidence. Please, Jenny, no matter what happens or is happening
when you read this letter, know that both your mother and I love
you and want you to be open and honest with us as long as you live.

My dad wrote this letter to me when I was six. Neither of us could
have imagined then how much I would struggle to overcome the
divorce's impact on my identity and sense of worth. Not only did the
divorce break my home, but it broke my heart and shattered my sense of

wholeness as well. Since the divorce cast doubt on the longevity of love, I wrestled to believe that I was capable or deserving of love. Because Mom and Dad put their desires first after their divorce, I could never quite believe that someone would make *me* a priority. Growing up, I doubted that my parents really wanted me to be a part of their new families because I felt like the leftover reminder of the failure of their old one.

As an adult, I've doubted that the guy I liked would ask me out, and if he did, I doubted that he'd still be interested enough to ask me out again. As a result I would often jeopardize relationships before the other person had the opportunity to reject me. I would deny my feelings of attraction because the thought of needing someone terrified me. I couldn't imagine that the man I would want to marry would want to marry me. My worst fear is that when I finally meet my Mr. Wonderful, he'll ulti-mately decide that the hard work of figuring out my family—and me!—isn't worth the effort. Even in my friendships, I am tempted to assume a relationship inequity—that my friends would mean more to me than I do to them.

When Angela, a twenty-five-year-old single woman, learned I was writing this book, she sought me out to tell me her story. She was nearly giddy in her enthusiasm to have her hurts affirmed at long last. "No one seems to understand why I wrestle so much. I know that something's not right, but I can't quite tell you what it is. I see it in my relationships…or at least my attempts at relationships." Angela went on to talk about a recent string of dates that never led to anything serious. "All these guys look great on paper, but I can't seem to make things work. When I see these same guys settle down with other women, I can't help but think that I'm the problem. What's so wrong with me that I seem utterly unlovable?"

Because Angela's definition of wholeness required the love of someone else, she found herself in an endless chase for the affections of another. When I asked her what she hoped a book for adult children of divorce would show her, she became emotional as she stumbled through her words, "I just want to know that I *can* know what it means to be whole. The divorce that was supposed to bring peace happened fifteen years ago, but there's *still* so much manipulation and lying and bad-mouthing in my family. I'm constantly changing myself to be a better person...one that doesn't get caught in all this drama. I guess what I really want to know is, is it possible to be who I am and still be loved?"

Angela's question strikes at the heart of our hope. To become whole, many of us will need to reconcile our emotional reality with the spiritual reality God presents to us in His Word. More definitively, we become whole as we exchange the perception of ourselves that our pasts have presented for the identities we have as much-loved sons and daughters of God.

While we do indeed come from broken homes, as believers we belong to a Daddy who is capable of restoring our shattered lives. However, since it took a lifetime for us to perfect the coping mechanisms we've learned to rely on, it will take some time to shed these reactions and heal. It will take time before we can get our hearts to embrace the love that God offers us, and it will take even more time before we allow this love to become part of our identities. It may go against everything we *feel* is right, but the end result is emotional and spiritual wholeness.

Just as a doctor prescribes a painful treatment to produce a more favorable prognosis, we must take a hard look at where we've been so we can change where we're going. When it comes to wholeness, many of us feel as though we're aiming in the dark at a moving target. This chapter will help you turn on the light and focus your aim.

What It Means to Be Whole

Stormie Omartian, author of *Lord, I Want to Be Whole,* defines emotional health as "having total peace about who you are, what you're doing, and where you're going, both individually and in relationship to those around you. In other words, it's feeling totally at peace about the past, present and future of your life."[1]

In chapter 9, we'll use the analogy of snapshots to create new models for understanding the concepts divorce has tainted. When the triggers of our past threaten our future, we can refer to these snapshots as a way of helping us picture what we are seeking to create for the album of our life. Sorting through the snapshots of wholeness, we discover this description of a whole person:

A Whole Person Acknowledges the Impact of the Past on the Present—but Is Not Victimized by That Reality

You took a step toward wholeness when you decided to read this book. Healing our hurts takes hard work, but this process will keep us from repeating the pain of the past in our present partnerships.

A Whole Person Realizes That Perfection Is Not Possible— but Intentionally Moves Toward Healing and Holiness

Striving for perfection will not bring the satisfaction we seek. We won't feel better about ourselves by being good, doing things right, controlling our circumstances, or avoiding conflict. However, when we embrace the grace God generously gives us, we can drop the drive to base our worth on works and instead relish and reflect the compassionate character of Christ.

A Whole Person Knows His or Her Strengths and Limitations— and Accepts Both As Starting Points for Growth

"Hi. My name is Bob, and I'm an alcoholic." Alcoholics Anonymous sponsors will tell you that this much-mocked admission is a powerful first step toward authenticity and recovery. Acknowledging the truth about ourselves brings freedom. When we are no longer hiding behind the mask of what we think we should be, we are free not only to be who we truly are but to begin to become the person we want to be.

Instead of being truthful about our needs, we learned to accommodate our parents' desires by stuffing and stifling our own. We have believed the lie that to name our hurts is to place blame and demonstrate ingratitude for our parents' efforts to buffer the pain their split inevitably caused. Continuing to deny the divorce's ramifications will not make them go away. Just as the alcoholic needs to understand the triggers that tempt him or her to drink, we must be willing to recognize and disarm the triggers of our trauma. (We will talk more about triggers in chapter 8.)

A Whole Person Can Articulate His or Her Needs and Feelings—and Ask for Help Without Manipulation

Manipulation stems from distrust. We don't believe that people will help us or look out for us simply out of the kindness of their hearts, so we butter them up or shame, blame, or guilt-trip them into doing what we want them to do. Ironically, most people would be happy to help if we would simply ask in a straightforward manner.

In relationships, we resort to manipulation when we are unable to articulate our needs and desires. We rely on our assumptions of how others will respond and approach them from the defensive. Whole people know themselves well enough to know what they want and need and are able to form healthy attachments with others who can meet their needs and whose needs they can meet.

When Travis and Becca married, both brought emotional baggage from their broken homes. At twenty-one and twenty respectively, the couple brought a joint subconscious desire to find a complete sense of self from the other. Three short years later, they were on the brink of breaking up. Despite their die-hard desire to avoid divorce, they realized too late that they had based their understanding of each other on projection rather than truth. While they did share the same needs and desires for completion, they assumed similarities instead of taking the time to discover each other's uniqueness. They were disappointed that the other could not live up to the idealistic image they had conjured up of the perfect spouse. As shortcomings were revealed, they were both ill-equipped to adjust and so they took the easy route to resentment. Instead of viewing those shortcomings as opportunities to grow together, they felt betrayed by the other's humanity.

When we don't know who we are or what we need, we can be tempted to emotionally use others as we "try on" a variety of personalities. To better understand what this looks like, imagine this scenario. A woman wanders into a shoe store. She's not sure if she even needs a new pair of shoes, but since she's in the area she decides to look around. As she walks the aisles, she tries on sandals, mules, heels, tennis shoes, pumps, boots, slippers, steel toes, and spikes. She moves along slowly because she's trying on shoes of all colors and styles. In the meantime, another shopper enters the store. An active volleyball player, she knows she needs tennis shoes with ankle support. She has a favorite brand, and her league requires her to wear white. Within minutes she is able to find a few options and quickly make her decision.

When we apply this scenario to our relationships, we can see that by taking time to get to know who we are, on our own, we can better recognize the type of partner and friend that would best complement us. People are too important for us to treat them as just another shoe in the store.

A Whole Person Seeks to Enhance Others' Lives—but Doesn't Expect Others to Make His or Her Life Complete

In their book *Relationships,* Drs. Les and Leslie Parrott state, "If you try to find intimacy with another person before achieving a sense of identity on your own, all your relationships become an attempt to complete yourself."[2] They define this pattern as the compulsion for completion.

While not nearly as romantic as Hollywood would have us believe, we can't look to others to complete us or we will ultimately use them and not serve them, connect with them, or find our life enhanced by them. We become whole by deriving our identity from something that is stable and unchanging, not from relationships that evolve with the seasons of life.

When we look to others to complete or define us, we place expectations on them that only God can meet. Are you looking to God to fulfill your needs for completion and love, or are you expecting your spouse or seeking a spouse to do so? No one can possibly handle that responsibility! By learning to love God totally and completely, we throw out our fantasies of perfect human love, and we learn what true love is.

The process of establishing healthy relationships can be likened to a trip to the grocery store. Though we need food to survive, we are more likely to make the healthiest purchases when we avoid shopping on an empty stomach. If we seek relationships to complete us, we approach them with a selfish agenda. If we engage in relationships satisfied in the value and worth we receive in Christ, we are able to fully give ourselves more completely and, in an ironic twist, make the intimate connections we yearn to find.

A Whole Person Can Give Selflessly—and Be Other-Focused

When we are fully confident in our intrinsic value—a person who is loved by God and created in His image—we can truly be other-focused. Our love for others overflows from the love we have received from God. Our relationships can then enhance our being rather than define it. We aren't looking to others to fill our cup. Instead, because our cup is overflowing, we seek to fill the cups of others.

BECOMING WHOLE

Taking into consideration that achieving emotional wholeness is a process, how do we become the person we've just described? Our healing process involves a textured complexity that cannot be broken down into several simplistic steps. However, we work toward continual closure using these processing points.

Go to God for Healing

If you want to become whole, you need God's help. He can bring to light those beliefs and behaviors that need to change. Not only that, but in the process of helping you make those adjustments, He can make you complete. As you pray and seek wholeness, ask God to guide you. Ask Him for the desire and strength to do the things you already know to do, such as grieving your losses and releasing resentment. Ask Him to reveal the things that may still be hidden, and then grieve those losses as well. Ask Him to bring people into your life who will love you well and give you the nurturing you need. Cooperate with God in this process, and He will honor your desire for healing and wholeness.

Examine Your Emotional Inheritance

I have friends who know their parents' history almost as well as those who lived it because those family stories are fondly retold time and time again on anniversaries and special occasions. I can't access that warm sense of shared history as easily, but I do have my parents' journal, which provides an incredibly personal glimpse into their lives and marriage. The journal, in some ways, is the "Dad and Mom" I dreamed of. In the innocence of their early relationship, I find hope.

As the years go by, their journal continues to beckon me. When I entered my first romantic relationship, I again read the journal, seeing my parents for the first time as peers. I wondered how in four short months they went from strangers to wedding arrangers, and just three months later took off on their honeymoon. I've long been amazed by how early they discussed marriage. I wonder if for them, the early discussion was motivated by a desire to conform to a societal expectation, while for me that first discussion is more a confirmation that I'm not wasting my time in the relationship.

As anniversaries passed, my parents took less time to make entries in the travelogue of their life. As I studied their notes, I looked for clues to help me understand why their love died. I have no doubt that I will continue to compare my life to theirs as I approach new life stages.

I think at some point in our adult life, we all must consider how our parents' marriage and divorce—and the behaviors we learned from that model—have affected our own ability to love and form lasting relationships. Generational sin is one spiritual ramification of our parents' choice. Without intentional intervention, we are likely to pass down those same traits to our children. My dad fleshed out this idea in his journal. He pointed out that just as the odds of getting cancer or having a stroke are greater if a family member succumbed to the disease, so the odds of seeing our own marriages end in divorce are increased when we come from broken homes. However, just as we can make healthy changes in our physical health to lower the risk of illness, we can make spiritual and emotional adjustments to increase the odds of beating the emotional and spiritual disease of divorce.

Each family has its own tendencies. In a physical sense, some families pass down genes carrying high metabolism, long legs, and thick hair. Other families endow slower, shorter, thinner genes. From an emotional/spiritual sense, families can pass down tendencies toward alcoholism, incest, abuse, or any other harmful behavior. So then, since we are not able to take an emotional DNA test to reveal our troublesome traits, how do we examine our emotional inheritance? Allow me to share an exercise that has helped me.

Take out a sheet of paper (or open your journal to a new page) and divide it into three columns. At the top of the first column, write the word *Trait*. Then list all the characteristics that come to mind when you think of each parent (have a separate list for each). For example, my mom made a conscious effort to teach me to value cultural diversity. She introduced me to different kinds of music and books. We watched movies about significant events, and when we traveled, we visited places that were outside our comfort zone for the experience of seeing life from a different perspective.

My dad is a humble man. From his quiet confidence I learned that it's more fulfilling when someone else pats you on the back than if you limber up to pat your own. My stepdad taught me the importance of knowledge. I appreciate how he drilled me on state capitals and U.S. presidents until I learned them. Before I ever sat behind the wheel of my first car, John helped me memorize all the parts of the engine.

As you reflect, think of your mom and dad in terms of their identities as people, parents, and partners. Say, for example, your mom was a creative person. As a parent, it meant she spent time playing with you, which made you feel loved. As a partner, her creativity helped her stretch the family budget.

Of course, since our parents are not perfect, you may find it easier to name their negative attributes. This is an important step in the process as well. So, list the negative traits your parents have modeled. Again, think of your mom and dad in terms of their identities as people, parents, and partners. Perhaps your dad was self-absorbed. As a person, that came out in the way he made decisions. That, in turn, affected his parenting style, as when he missed important events in your life to do something else, say, attend a ball game. That choice meant, as a partner, he spent money on game tickets when the family budget dictated that those funds should have gone to whittle down debt.

Take your time with this list. There's no deadline. In fact, you may want to consider keeping it handy for the rest of your life as new experiences present different lenses for reflection.

In the second column write, *How Do I Show This?* Consider how you may exhibit both the positive and the negative traits. If you are married, have your spouse help you with this inventory. If you are single, ask a trusted friend to work through the list with you. The objectivity of our loved ones may help reveal a continuity of character that we might miss on our own.

Be specific. Describe a situation that shows that trait in you. Write it down and read it out loud. As you note generational comparisons, consider alternatives to the tendencies you want to change. Label the third column, *What Should I Do Differently?*

In my own reflection, I realized I had inherited from my mom a tendency to internalize my decision-making process rather than invite others involved in the outcome to help me come to a resolution. In terms of her marriages, it seems to me that as Mom's dissatisfaction grew, so did her tendency to withdraw. As she internally considered the pros and cons of saving the marriage, her family was unaware of the depth of her pain. By the time Mom came to the conclusion that her marriages weren't worth saving, my dads were just realizing how seriously the marriages were damaged. While her independence has made her a successful survivor, I think it has hindered her ability to be truly intimate with her husbands. She missed the depth of satisfaction that comes when a marriage naturally flows back from seasons of dissatisfaction.

I see this tendency in my own life when I disengage from my friends during emotional times. I recognize that I've learned it's easier to be alone than to be vulnerable enough to allow others a full view of my unsorted emotions. I can think of two practical ways to reverse this tendency. First, I need to practice authenticity with my family of friends. I must not only tell them about this tendency, but I must be willing to share my confused feelings with them as honestly as I can articulate them, and then invite my friends to offer counsel based on truth and that which affirms our faith. This will help me build healthy friendships in the present, and it will also strengthen the relational patterns I *want* to bring into my marriage. Second, I need to submit my thoughts and feelings to God and humbly allow Him—and not my emotions—to direct my responses in a way that pleases Him and blesses me.

Mind Your Mind

As much as it may sometimes seem otherwise, divorce is something that happened *to* us, it *does not* define us. As an adult child of divorce, you may struggle to know and believe the truth about yourself. Secret fears may nag at the back of your mind, saying you're "damaged goods" or that you're bound to fall into your parents' patterns of behavior or that you aren't good enough to deserve God's best. These are lies!

It may take a long time before you can successfully thwart these thoughts from poisoning your identity. Be vigilant in your own defense and refuse to allow those wrong thoughts to root themselves in your psyche. When those thoughts attack, remind yourself of the truth: God loves you! He has never abandoned you! He desires good things for you as you seek to live according to His plan.

God's Word offers this hope, "We demolish arguments and every pretension that sets itself up against the knowledge of God, and we take captive every thought to make it obedient to Christ" (2 Corinthians 10:5). When wrong thoughts cross our minds, we have the choice either to dwell on them or banish them. We take our thoughts captive when we make them consistent with the truth Christ claims for us.

However, persistent thoughts may not go away simply because we want them to. For example, during one season of struggle, I wrestled with the thought that no one loved me. I knew this thought was not accurate, but it was persistent. At last, I decided to pray it into obedience. Every time that thought entered my mind, I prayed, "Dear Jesus, thank You for the truth that sets me free. Thank You for loving me so much that You died for me. Thank You for loving me so much that You created me with a purpose. Thank You for loving me so much that You gave me the ability to write and articulate my thoughts. Thank You for loving me so much that You gave me friends who are willing to spend time with me…" I would thus drown the lie with evidence of the opposite. After a while the truth finally sank in, and that thought has not been an issue since.

Treasure the Truth

As you seek wholeness, consider doing a study based on Neil Anderson's classic book *Victory Over the Darkness,* which has helped countless Christians realize the power of their identities in Christ. His thirty-six "Who Am I?" statements are often cited by believers who desire to treasure the truth of all God promises us.

In addition, take a look at your strengths. Each of us is uniquely created with specific talents, abilities, interests, and passions. How well do you know yourself? Can you define your identity independent of another person? What qualities make you a good friend or spouse? What talents or gifts do you have? Are you using them to serve your church and community? Pray for God to show you how He wants you to use those strengths, talents, and gifts for His glory.

Now think about your weaknesses. You may have learned some tendencies from your family that you'd be better off unlearning. What role did you play during the struggles at home? I was the perfectionist. I thought that if I had done everything right, my family would have stayed together. As a grown woman, I thought that if I never showed any weakness, I would be worthy of love. I had to learn to tell my friends when they hurt my feelings. What do *you* need to learn?

Define Your Direction

When we look to others to complete us, we abdicate our responsibility to define our own direction. We make decisions based on our desire to be acceptable to others instead of being true to Christ's calling on our life. And the kind of people that allow us to depend on them that way are not likely to be the kind of people we can truly depend on. We need to be healthy to attract healthy people.

Several years ago, I made a list of ten life goals that I needed to work on. I wrote them in the front of my Bible as a covenant that I would not allow a romantic relationship to develop until those goals had taken root in my life. As time went on, they came to define the woman I felt God wanted me to become, regardless of my marital status.

Lord, help me to be committed to…

- *spiritual growth.* I want to focus on my relationship with You, have a consistent quiet time, and develop intimate relationships that draw me closer to You.

- *financial stability.* I want to live on a workable budget and have no debt (other than a mortgage) so that my husband and I will not need my income to pay our bills.

- *emotional health.* I want to strive to have a healthy emotional life. I realize this is an ongoing process as a result of prayer, knowledge wise counsel, accountability, and effort.

- *a realistic view of marriage.* I want to know and understand the challenges and stages of marriage, be committed to the long haul, and find mentors.

- *physical fitness.* I want to do the best with what I have.

- *godly friendships.* I want to seek accountability and support and develop an intimate family of friends because I know a husband cannot fulfill all my needs all the time.

- *purity.* I want to remain a virgin until I marry and keep mentally pure.

- *being loyal.* I want to develop a supportive personality that admires strengths and encourages people during trials. I need to overcome the urge to run.

- *ministry.* I want to use my God-given gifts to serve.

- *a life vision.* I want to establish a godly heritage, make an eternal difference, and find joy in life regardless of my circumstances.

These life goals have helped me regain a proper perspective in times of struggle and indecision, because they offer tangible areas on which to focus. As we make our way through life, different temptations will try to distract us from our life goals. While some of these temptations may actually be good, such as marriage, children, and financial security, I have found that when I focus on these "floating desires," I lose my sense of direction. My life goals offer a singleness of purpose and an objective measure of the compatibility of a person or plan with my calling.

Spend time in prayer and seek the counsel of others to define the character God wants you to develop. Then begin your journey with assurance in your steps. As you intentionally seek emotional health, you will begin to develop the characteristics that will enhance the future you desire. But first you must learn to trust, which is the subject of the next chapter.

Word

I will restore you to health and heal your wounds.
(Jeremiah 30:17)

Reflect
- Take an afternoon to reflect and do the "Traits" exercise explained on pages 109–111.
- How would you describe the current season of your life— Self-imposed? Productive? Depressing? Fulfilling? Based in fear? Anticipatory? What changes could you make to make better use of this time?
- Do you believe that God has a purpose for your life? What do you think it is? What are you doing to fulfill that call?

- What three life goals most direct your decisions? What are the floating desires that distract you from those goals?
- What positive attributes can you contribute to a relationship? What are your weaknesses? Make a list of character traits you hope to possess. Commit to developing those traits now.
- If you are single, do you have a clear idea of what kind of person would best complement you? Do the people you find romantically attractive possess the characteristics you desire in a spouse? Do you possess the traits that would be desirable to the kind of person you wish to attract?

Challenge

If you have not intentionally considered the person you want to be, take time to create "A Description of [Your Name]." Include your core values, key character qualities, and life goals.

If you are single, this is a good time to consider what kind of person would best complement you. Consider creating a list with ten character traits of such a person. Use this list as a prayer guide for the times your thoughts are drawn toward marriage.

If you are married, take time with your spouse to consider what kind of marriage you'd like to create together. We'll talk more about how to develop a healthy, whole sense of "we" in your marriage in chapter 9.

Read

Emotions: Can You Trust Them? by James Dobson (Regal, 1995)
Lord, I Want to Be Whole by Stormie Omartian (Nelson, 2000)
Victory Over the Darkness by Neil T. Anderson (Regal, 1990)

7

Learn to Trust

Effect: *The experience of divorce hinders our ability to trust and assess the trustworthiness of others.*

Hope: *We can choose to connect in healthy relationships with people worthy of our trust.*

Thirty-three and single, Ken would like to be in a close relationship with someone. He has friends but can't figure out why his connections aren't as deep or strong as the relationships his friends seem to have with others. He explained, "I feel like I'm walking around the perimeter of intimacy. I could give you a textbook answer to describe a healthy relationship, but for whatever reason, I can't seem to get past the periphery and put skin on my theories."

Ken's parents have been divorced for nearly twenty years. Both have remarried and settled into new routines. When asked to describe why he thought his parents divorced, he said, "You know, I really think my parents had more of a roommate relationship. The only time I ever saw them even touch each other was a quick kiss during the greeting time at church. They just aren't real affectionate. I don't remember ever receiving a hug from my mom or dad, though I did get an occasional slap on the back or handshake to acknowledge an accomplishment."

When Ken was fourteen, his dad began an affair. The stoic father Ken knew transformed into an affectionate flirt, utterly unconcerned with appearances or the embarrassment his son was feeling. After the divorce,

Ken moved in with his dad, who gushed that he finally felt alive as he detailed years of dissatisfaction in the bedroom.

The revelation about his parents' sexuality came at the time Ken was beginning to deal with his own emerging urges. Because his father's affections were only expressed toward his new girlfriend, Ken learned to connect affection with misplaced sexuality. As a result, Ken stifled his own sexual and emotional development. Underlying every action was a desire *not* to become his dad.

As an adult, Ken struggles to develop intimate connections. His friendships are focused on the superficial, and he avoids dating altogether. Not only does Ken have a hard time trusting others, he doesn't trust himself, either.

How Divorce Affects Our Ability to Trust

Everyone wants to be wanted, needed, enjoyed, accepted, known, and loved. Our longing for belonging is an innate and undeniable part of our makeup, but our family's failure to give us consistent connection can warp our framework for intimacy. Our fears of being dismissed, let down, betrayed, abandoned, or rejected stifle our willingness to risk authenticity and vulnerability as an adult. We send mixed "Come here!/Go away!" signals as we vacillate between our conflicting impulses of revelation and restraint. As we learned in the previous chapter, adult children of divorce often enter relationships asking, "What can I get from this person?" instead of "What can I give this person?"

Pioneer psychologist Erik Erikson outlined a progression of development to explain human behavior. He concluded that each psychosocial stage includes a crisis that must be resolved in order to successfully move to the next level of development. If a child skips a stage or fails to resolve the crisis, the child will continue to struggle with the task of that stage until it is faced and finished.

Not surprisingly, the very first task is developing a sense of trust. According to Dictionary.com, trust is the "firm reliance on the integrity, ability or character of a person or thing."[1] Trust implies a faith that the object of our trust will not let us down. When our parents divorce, we often experience an emotional regression to this first stage of development because the anchor of our security—a home with both parents—has come loose in the storm. The divorce represents a major trust violation, whether or not we were able to articulate or acknowledge it at the time. Our issues with trust make us vulnerable to several relationship pitfalls.

An Inability to Accurately Assess Relationships

If our parents told us that everything was fine despite the obvious tension or overt oppression in our home, we may have shut down our intuitive interpretation of the situation to make it compute with what we were told. However, if our parents ultimately divorced ("Aha! Things were not okay."), we don't automatically regain our ability to accurately assess our relationships. As adults, this disconnect can show up as we misinterpret relationships by assuming a commitment or interest that isn't there. That's what Maria did in her friendship with Brandon.

Both college seniors, Maria and Brandon ate meals together, talked on the phone daily, and often socialized together. Brandon never made any romantic moves toward Maria, and when they talked about their relationship, he told her how much he appreciated that they could just be friends.

As time went on, Maria began to develop romantic feelings for Brandon. Even though he continued to clearly express his platonic feelings for her, she told herself that he really did want more. As graduation loomed and Maria began to imagine a postcollege life, she began dropping hints to Brandon that conveyed the change in her intentions. He did not take the hint. Sinking further into denial, she stopped presenting their relationship as platonic and began lacing her comments to others with innuendo that she had a romance with Brandon. She rationalized that his lack of romantic expression was simply respect for her physical boundaries. A week before graduation, Maria was crushed as Brandon confronted her with the choice to either be content as friends or end the friendship.

An inability to trust can also present itself in relational extremes: Either we become so guarded that we don't trust anyone, or we trust too easily and do not recognize when we are being used.

Too Guarded

Twenty-six-year-old Heather acknowledged the depth of her distrust. She wrote,

> If I'm in a relationship with someone, and I don't think it's going anywhere, I break it off quickly. I used to think this was a good way to guard my heart, but now I'm not so sure. I probably break things off too quickly, as soon as I see something I don't like. I guess it sounds harsh, but I figure that if they aren't perfect, they can't be trusted with my fragile bag of emotions. Honestly, I just wish I knew how to know when someone is actually trustworthy.

In my own life, when it came to romantic relationships, I would bombard my suitors with a laundry list of introspective questions. I thought that if I covered all the bases and he answered in the right way, then I could relax and enjoy building a relationship with a safe person. What I eventually learned is that rushing someone through the ritual of self-disclosure short-circuits the development of the trust I'm hoping to build.

Not Guarded Enough

Julie was eighteen when her parents divorced. Since Julie and her mom had always been close, Julie became her mother's primary advocate and confidant after the split. She prided herself on her ability to meet her mom's emotional needs, even though the information her mom shared with her violated healthy parent-child boundaries. Julie decided to forgo her scholarship to a college out of state so she could stay close to her mom. After all, Julie rationalized, "Who could take better care of Mom than I?"

The students in Julie's residence hall were drawn to her maturity and ability to keep their secrets. It wasn't until she faced a crisis of her own that she realized how one-sided her relationships really were.

Julie fell victim to relationship inequity. Because her intimate connections did not include mutual reciprocity, mutual self-disclosure, and mutual commitment, those relationships were unable to support Julie when she was the one who needed help. Julie took the caretaker coping mechanism she learned with her mother into her other relationships. As a result, Julie's "friendships" were based only on what Julie could give; they did not include the giving of others *to Julie*. Julie was not guarded enough in her boundaries to limit the emotional expectations of others.

While a person like Julie sponges up the feelings of those around her, the flip side of not being guarded enough includes those who want so much to be heard that they spew all their emotional stuff on anyone who will lend an ear. They may see themselves as open and vulnerable, but their lack of restraint reveals an inability to create realistic give-and-take in a relationship. These relationships demonstrate an inequity of mutuality as well, because intimacy is assumed prematurely.

When we consider how long it has taken us not only to acknowledge our hurts but also to begin to process them, we can see how unfair it is to dump our unedited diatribes on people we don't know well. Not only is it unrealistic to expect that they can process everything we say, but it is rather improbable that they would be able to offer any practical assistance.

Learning appropriate trust requires that we learn how to recognize who is and is not trustworthy and that we maintain a healthy balance of restraint and revelation. At some point in our healing, we need to re-establish our anchor of security, that object of reliable trust. We must find someone worthy of trust so that we might safely attempt to trust again.

DEFINING TRUSTWORTHINESS

Dogs are often described as man's best friend because they personify trustworthiness. In fact, a friend of mine works for a ministry that uses animal therapy to help abused kids learn to trust again. The animal functions as a bridge whereby a child can begin to trust people and love again by first opening up to and trusting an animal.

Recently, my dog, Bailey Grace, turned two. As I reflected on how my life has changed since I adopted this adorable fluffball, I realized just how much God has used her to teach me to love and trust. At first when I talked about some cute way Bailey amused me, if my listener didn't share my enthusiasm, my feelings would sometimes get hurt. From an intellectual perspective, I could understand why they wouldn't equate my Bailey adventures with the stories they shared about their kids. What I more recently realized is that my excitement stemmed from the emotional healing in my life as Bailey increased my capacity to love.

Of course, it's much easier to love a pet than a person. So how do we then move into trusting relationships with people? We must create a clear picture of what we're looking for. To do that, we must ask ourselves, "What does a trustworthy person look like?" Trustworthy people have the following traits:

- *Authenticity.* There is a continuity to their character.
- *Vulnerability.* They are willing to risk self-disclosure, both the good and not-so-good.
- *Loyalty.* They are willing and able to act sacrificially in your best interest even when it isn't convenient or fun (helping during a move, offering comfort in hard times, caretaking and cleaning when you're sick).

- *Grace.* They are willing and able to forgive and move on.
- *Honesty.* They are realistic and transparent in their assessment of self and others.
- *Positive influence.* They support and encourage healing and integrity.

Obviously no one is all of these things all the time. We all have our bad days and our less-than-ideal moments. However, the trustworthy person acknowledges his or her imperfections and deals with them by seeking forgiveness when needed and by being committed to consistent and intentional growth.

As we find people in our life who exhibit these qualities, we can make an intentional choice to trust them with ourselves, even if it feels risky. That's how Ken is gradually learning to trust others. Even though he has been fearful of trusting others, Ken has a lot of confidence in his ability to intellectually understand a topic such as, "what a healthy relationship looks like." So Ken is learning to trust others on an *emotional* level by using his intellectual competency. For example, when he meets someone who is trustworthy according to the above list, he tunes in to what he's thinking when the walls start coming up, and then he tears down those barriers with the truth.

Internally the process looks like this: Ken tells himself, "I do not want to be stuck in this pit any longer. I am choosing to push past this uncomfortable feeling, and I am going to share who I am with this person. This person demonstrates authenticity, vulnerability, loyalty, grace, honesty, and positive influence; therefore, it is okay to share my thoughts with her."

ASSESSING THE HEALTH AND DEPTH OF OUR RELATIONSHIPS

As children of divorce, we have had to fend for ourself emotionally and/or physically for a portion of our life. We've learned to be independent out of necessity. We've learned to protect our heart, and in the process, our heart may have become so callous that we may not know how to let others in. We may hold others at a "safe" distance—close enough to interact, but not near enough that they can influence or hurt us. Though we may desperately want to love and be loved—to be interdependent—out of fear we may jeopardize our opportunities. If we want to heal and have satisfying and fulfilling relationships with others—including lifelong spouses—we must embrace the "we" of the relationship over individual preferences. We must cultivate relationships that value vulnerability, shared goals, and togetherness. Learning to trust means learning to be interdependent.

This all may sound good in theory, but how do we go from nonexistent or unhealthy relationships to close relationships that are healthy? The answer lies in understanding the nature and purpose of friendships and the various levels of relationships.

Understanding the Nature and Purpose of Friendship

As we become aware of our need for intimate friendships, we may realize that we have closed ourselves off from others in an effort to avoid getting hurt. John Gray, the author of *Men Are from Mars, Women Are from Venus,* refers to this mostly masculine tendency as "going into our caves."[2] The problem with this, of course, is that the love we seek isn't going to enter our caves without an invitation. Proverbs 27:17 tells us that as iron sharpens iron, so one person sharpens another. We simply cannot grow without the influence and interaction of others. Without relationships, we become dull.

It will take time to develop the trust necessary to be successful in our most intimate relationships, but even before we reveal our heart, we can be wise by carefully selecting friends who reflect the qualities of a trustworthy person. Since we become like the company we keep, we should choose to be friends with those who share our values and goals. Proverbs 12:26 explains it this way: "A righteous man is cautious in friendship, but the way of the wicked leads them astray." This isn't to say we avoid those who don't share our values, but we choose to focus our energy on relationships that encourage and energize us, rather than on those that drain us or conflict with our consciences. As we spend the majority of our time with those closest to us emotionally, we are encouraged to become the person we wish and need to be. Grounded and confident, we have the resources to reach out to others with a genuine other-focus because we are not dependent on them to fulfill us.

Our capacity to accurately assess the health and depth of our relationships grows as we gain an accurate understanding of the nature of relationships. Many people mistakenly equate permanence with successful relationships. The truth is, not all relationships are meant to be permanent. Some people are brought into our life for a reason, a brief but meaningful exchange that marks a memorable moment in our journey. Others remain with us for a season. When friends from school begin to feel as distant emotionally as they are physically, the distance does not erase our time of intimacy. It is progression, not betrayal. Precious few enter our life for the remainder of our days. Just as it is not possible to maintain a large number of intimate relationships for a lifetime, it is not practical, or healthy, to pour all of ourselves into every relationship.

Recognizing the Levels of Relationships

Christians, especially, can fall for the myth that all relationships should have the same depth of intimacy, vulnerability, and loyalty. But that's just not true. We were not created with the capacity to give everything we have to everyone we meet. We do not give the person in the grocery line the same access to our heart that we give our husband. We do not put the welfare of a coworker above our child's.

Consider a raindrop falling to the sea. The point of greatest impact and depth is in the center, that is, the exact place where the raindrop hits the water. Circling around that point are increasingly larger, but more shallow ripples. In the ocean of our life, our point of greatest impact and depth—our most intimate relationship—is our relationship with God. Our ripples of relationship spread from that one aquatic indentation. We can use this analogy to understand how the relationship ripples in our life reflect various levels of intimacy.

The outer ripple of our relationship circle is made up of the Multitude of Acquaintances whose paths cross ours: folks at church, coworkers, people in the grocery store, or those who sit next to us in class. Typically, our life with these folks has only one point of intersection—church, work, school, or our neighborhood—and our crossing is unintentional. Our obligation to and expectation of those in this circle is typically not much more than a hello or a friendly wave. Sometimes, circumstances may create a second and more enduring point of connection. The person in class works on a project with us, and we meet at her apartment. The person at work shares a table with us at a corporate event, and our conversation strays past small talk.

Once we discover a shared interest with someone, that person generally moves into our Fellowship Friend circle. The depth of involvement is still shallow, but the potential is there for more. We both enjoy volleyball or dancing or Scrabble or something that leads us to keep each other's numbers handy in case we get the urge to do that activity. If we host a party, these are the people we are likely to invite.

It is not appropriate or healthy for us to be vulnerable and trusting with people at these levels of relationship ripples, because real intimacy doesn't begin to form until our friends move to the Comfortable Confidant level. At this point, we have discovered that we share common interests and values. We are now willing to pursue our interactions with them. We join the same league or class or Bible study. We take the same route as we jog, or we hit the gym at the same time. As we spend time together, we enjoy a mutual and equitable reciprocity.

Most of the people in this ripple are peers, but some may be older, wiser adults who are willing to step into a more parental role, especially when physical or emotional distance prevents us from seeking the counsel of our own parents. These more mature individuals have entered our ripples based on their experience and expertise, their character and maturity, and their willingness to engage in our life. Their lives exhibit the qualities of a trustworthy person. We might seek their counsel with the major decisions of life: choosing a career path, purchasing a home, making financial decisions, and even selecting a spouse. They don't tell us what to do, but they can ask us questions and offer their opinions based on what they know of us and the values that direct our decisions. Because their life experiences are broader than our peers, they may be able to see our circumstances more clearly than our peers who are viewing life from our same vantage point.

Each level of relationship will have fewer participants. It takes time to involve ourselves with others. We have a limit to our emotional capital, so we limit our investments to those we feel offer the best return for our risk. For this reason, very few people will enter—and remain in—our most inner circle, that of our Accountable Advisors, over the course of a lifetime. And, as I have learned, rarely will these relationships develop without intentional initiative.

When we are mindful of the various levels of relationship, we gain great freedom to create appropriate boundaries—not everyone needs to be our "best" friend—and allow our friendships to develop depth over time.

Psychologist Larry Crabb asserts in his book *Connecting* that most of the emotional needs met through counseling could be avoided altogether if believers engaged in one another's lives. Accountability is the voluntary, intentional willingness to allow another to engage fully in our life in a relationship built on trust, loyalty, and commitment.

As I mentioned earlier, I have purposefully entered into a covenant friendship with four other women. To signify our intentionality, we have developed our own traditions and habits of interaction, including the creation of our own name, The Cloud of Witnesses, based on Hebrews

12:1. For short, and for fun, we adopted the affectionate term the COWs.

We have celebrated birthdays and holidays together, we've prayed with one another for our spouses or future spouses, and we have celebrated the addition of "COW-boys" to our family circle. We've been intentional about sharing our struggles and successes, our goals and our goings-on. As we've come to know and appreciate our individual personalities, we've learned how to confront and challenge one another to reach our individual goals and continually grow in Christlike character.

These friends understand they are my family of choice. When trigger events aim to make a mess of my emotions, they are the ones who step in and remind me of the truth: I am loved, I am valuable, and I am needed. On holidays and my birthday, when I battle the bombardment of loneliness and longing, they step up to make me feel like the priority I want to be. They show me that I'm needed when I forget I have gifts, and they shower me with the love I'm afraid to ask for.

When one of us gets dumped, we all feel the disappointment of those dying dreams. When one of us gets engaged, we all celebrate the addition of a new brother. These women are my safe place. In times of joy they are the ones with whom I celebrate and praise God. In times of struggle they are the ones who are strong for me, checking in on me when my tendency is to check out. When I am tempted, they are the ones who ask the hard questions and remind me again of my goals. They are the ones with whom feelings are free from censure: We laugh when it's silly, we cry when it hurts, we wrestle when it's difficult, and we celebrate when it resolves. These close friends are women of character and grace, and because of them I become more consistent in my own character and grace. More than anything else, they have given me confidence and hope that I am learning what it means to love well, commit well, and be well.

My relationships with these women are not successful because they are promised to be permanent. Already continents have come between us, and though we may not see one another daily or regularly, these relationships are successful because they are intentionally intimate. Time will tell how long we will share our journey together, but in the meantime, these women are helping me learn to trust and better understand the nature and health of my other relationships.

One of my COWs, Rachael, has taken a more active role in my life than the others. In addition to being a one-time roommate, she has also become my *primary accountability partner.* Once a week, Rachael and I touch base for a time of transparent sharing. For several years, we have used this time to read together, brainstorm solutions to our struggles, remind each other of the truth that supersedes our untruthful thoughts, encourage each other, and pray for and with each other.

God has used my dear, compassionate friend to help me winnow truth from lies when my heart hurts. When my perspective is skewed, Rachael helps me see more clearly. She and I ask each other pointed questions about our lives, and we expect to both give and receive honest answers. Regardless of how we spend our time together, the ultimate function of our friendship is to guide each other toward greater godliness. We encourage those things that are consistent with that character, and we confront each other by pointing out and helping the other replace those things that conflict with our goals.

Not every friendship is an accountability relationship, because it's not possible to create and maintain the healthy environment necessary for accountability in every friendship. Accountability requires a willingness to be utterly honest with another regarding our thoughts, actions, intentions, and motivations. It requires a willingness to be transparent and nondefensive when we share or are asked to share about our life. The person to whom we are accountable shares an obligation as well: to be loyal, to honor confidentiality, to be committed to our betterment and growth, and to support us unconditionally even as our ugly side is exposed. Our accountability partner, in relationship to this type of interaction, must be utterly other-focused. And as an accountability *partner*, we must strive for this same level of other-focus as we regard our partner's best interest.

Some cringe at the concept of accountability because they fear that it involves judging. In reality, accountability is the process of developing healthy boundaries and expectations as we learn to know and be known, to love and be loved, to stick around when it isn't easy, and to consider the needs of another as carefully as our own. It's allowing another person to love you the way you've always wanted to be loved. Through accountability we learn to trust others so that we can form intimate, healthy relationships. Accountability relationships take up the slack for the lessons our divorced parents might have failed to impart or for the inaccurate lessons they may have intentionally or inadvertently taught us. Accountability relationships are guardrails on the road to a healthy future.

THE RIPPLES OF ROMANCE

When it comes to our romantic pursuits, the inner ripples of our relationship circles can provide a safeguard for us. Because we have been intentional in developing relationships marked by authenticity, we have people in place to provide perspective as we pursue a permanent partner.

What often happens when people date without these safeguards is that the object of affection moves from the outer ripple to the inner ripple very quickly. Without patience and accountability, we can get too close too soon by allowing the romantic interest to skip over the stages of relational development, thus bringing that person prematurely into our center circle. At the same time, we often push our established relationships aside as we create our own enclosed circle with the person we are dating.

You can probably think of a close friend who has done this at some point. Do you remember how it made you feel? Pushed away? Ignored? Abandoned? That's the idea. Not only does the individual miss out on the counsel of those who have established their trust and willingness to look out for that person's best interest, but by pushing those in the inner circle away, he or she is setting the table for a banquet of resentment. If things don't work out with the intended, what happens? The object of affection is gone, and the Accountable Advisors have been pushed away to the outer limits. Instead of offering condolence and support, those who are best set up to minister to the individual have to wrestle with resentment.

My early experiences with romance took the opposite approach. A few months into my faith, a seminar on courtship convicted me. God revealed the idolatry in my heart: I looked to guys to validate my self-worth. My natural inclination, wherever I was, whatever I was doing, was to look around and see if there was anyone who caught my eye. What I sensed God asking me to do that day was to give Him the next year. During that time, I would not pursue any relationship but His. I would use the time and energy I had devoted to dating or pursuing relationships to "date" and pursue my relationship with God. Instead of seeking my value and worth from guys, I would use that year to learn to see myself through God's eternal perspective.

What started as a pure desire became a comfortable pattern of avoidance. While I wouldn't go back now and do anything differently, I recognized years later that I allowed that decision to be a convenient excuse to avoid learning healthy ways of relating to guys. One year to God became two, two became three, and three became a way of life that used a false spirituality to mark my fear. For the most part, after that year off, I viewed men as nonentities. If I wasn't open to dating them, I didn't see the point in getting to know them past the Fellowship Friend level. As much as I struggled to understand God's unconditional love, human love seemed an unattainable goal for me. I didn't trust myself to give my heart to another, and I didn't trust anyone enough to believe that his heart wouldn't come with conditions.

I developed a complicated duality that both protected my heart and allowed me to play at love. Because I couldn't believe that someone might actually like me, I figured that the next best thing was to like someone safe, that is, someone who neither pursued me nor pursued anyone else. I would develop a friendship with a man, carefully denying any feelings of attraction. Though I wasn't cognizant of my motivation, I convinced myself that the thrill of liking someone was as much as I could expect. It took a long time to see how manipulative I was in these situations. I regret that I missed out on many opportunities to authentically learn together, grow together, or serve together with guy friends because of this selfish subtext.

God used a series of men to teach me to view the guys in my life as brothers. It took the marriages of many of my friends to force me to build genuine, healthy friendships with men—relationships that were not romantic, but involved meaningful interactions. As I've become intentional about developing intimacy in my ripples of relationships, I've been able to venture into the realm of romance with more confidence because I know I have the accountability of friends I trust. Over time, I've learned that love is both more complicated than I once believed and yet more simple. I've learned that it's not enough to love someone who doesn't love you back, and it's not fair to accept the love of someone you can't love in return. I've learned that a broken heart doesn't mean I can't love well, and even though my future is unknown, I thank God for giving me the courage to put training wheels on this timid heart of mine.

When we don't rush through the ripples of relationship, the levels provide road signs to guide us along a safer road to romance. A friendship-with-potential grows slowly, stopping at each stage and building intimacy through balanced doses of revelation and restraint.

Because we have already established trust with our Accountable Advisors, we invite them to offer counsel when needed and to step in when their objectivity enables them to see that our attention is misdirected or misinterpreted. We are better able to protect our heart because we are less likely to give it away to someone who has not asked for it. As we approach emotional, spiritual, and financial readiness for marriage, our Accountable Advisors can provide valuable insight regarding the characteristics we might seek in a partner, based on our personalities, preferences, and purposes in life.

Without this accountability, we often lack the objectivity to accurately assess our breakups. When we approach our relationships with a compulsion for permanence, we have a tendency to project attributes on another simply because we want to believe we've found "the one." When the relationship does not turn out the way we had planned, we think that our heartbreaker betrayed us or misled us, when what actually might have happened was that he knew himself well enough to know that the relationship was not ideal. We might perceive a breakup as a failure to find "the one," when in reality the parting of ways was a natural end to that particular relational trail.

When we don't expect others to complete us, we have the opportunity to experience great satisfaction and fulfillment in our romances, even if our partnerships don't end up to be permanent. Our relationships are not failures just because they don't lead to marriage, but we can cause them to be if we fail to learn what we have been brought together to teach one another.

TRUSTING OTHERS IN THE RACE OF LIFE

One of the highlights of my college experience was the annual Drake Relays. The weeklong festivities include the Iowa state high-school championship track-and-field meet, a collegiate tournament, and special invitation-only events featuring some of the best runners in the world. While only the winners' names are etched into medals, no competitor runs alone. In the months prior to the event, each contestant is spurred on by those entrusted to help the runner achieve his or her goal. Coaches, trainers, and teammates all play a part in the training process: Coaches challenge and push, trainers pay special attention to the health of the runners, and teammates provide a point of comparison. On the day of the meet, the cheers of the crowd remind the runners that many eyes are watching. In the heat of the moment, other runners and even cheers directed to the competition provide incentive to push ahead through the pain of their pursuit.

In the same way a runner critiques every aspect of his race, we, as Christians, can refer to this racing analogy to explain the lifelong process of spiritual transformation:

> Do you not know that in a race all the runners run, but only one gets the prize? Run in such a way as to get the prize. Everyone who competes in the games goes into strict training. They do it to get a crown that will not last; but we do it to get a crown that will last forever. Therefore I do not run like a man running aimlessly.... No, I beat my body and make it my slave so that after I have preached to others, I myself will not be disqualified for the prize. (1 Corinthians 9:24-27)

This analogy is especially fitting for us, as children of divorce, as we engage in the lifelong process of healing and allowing God to change us into people who are capable of livelong love and commitment. Hebrews 12:1 has become my theme verse in this regard: "Therefore, since we are surrounded by such a great cloud of witnesses, let us throw off everything that hinders and the sin that so easily entangles, and let us run with perseverance the race marked out for us."

Just as a runner looks to his trainer and coach to point out those mannerisms and habits that hinder his speed, we need the objective opinion of those committed to our success to help us learn to trust in healthy ways.

Word

Therefore, since we are surrounded by such a great cloud of witnesses, let us throw off everything that hinders and the sin that so easily entangles, and let us run with perseverance the race marked out for us. (Hebrews 12:1)

Reflect

- Do any of these statements reflect your relationship patterns? In what way does the description relate to you?
  - ▾ Trust is built in degrees. I have high expectations for those with whom I choose to enter relationships. Once trust is established, I am very loyal.
  - ▾ I tend to initiate the end of my relationships. I'd rather leave someone than be rejected or abandoned.
  - ▾ I tend to stay in long-term relationships. Anything is better than being alone.
- Who was the best friend you ever had, and what made that person such a good friend?
- Do your friends have characteristics that encourage or discourage trust? In what ways?
- When you think of the kind of intimate relationship you'd like to have with a friend, what do you envision that looking like—how do you interact physically and emotionally? What do you talk about? What's off-limits?
- What about a romantic relationship? What do you think needs to happen, on both your part and his (or hers), to create that kind of relationship?
- What does someone have to do to earn your trust? What does someone have to do to break it? Are your expectations fair?

- List the names of the people you would consider part of your ripples of relationship:
  - ▾ Fellowship Friends
  - ▾ Comfortable Confidants
  - ▾ Accountable Advisors
- Looking at your lists, are you satisfied with the distribution of your emotional resources? If not, what adjustments do you need to make?

Challenge

Consider the depth of your relationships. Do you have anyone with whom you would consider yourself truly accountable? If not, prayerfully contemplate your need for such a person (or persons) and determine your plan to propose it.

Read

Attachments by Tim Clinton and Gary Sibcy (Integrity Publishers, 2002)

Dropping Your Guard by Chuck Swindoll (Word, 1982)

Connecting by Larry Crabb (Word, 1997)

Mentoring by Bob Biehl (Broadman and Holman, 1997)

Relationships by Les and Leslie Parrott (Zondervan, 1998)

8

Anticipate Our Triggers

Effect: Situations and events can set up explosive emotions we don't understand.

Hope: By anticipating our triggers, we can minimize their impact on us.

Twenty-one-year-old Lisa didn't think the divorce was a big deal. Her parents broke up when she was three, and by the time she was ten, both had remarried. Most of her friends' parents were divorced as well, and she just figured that the bimonthly parental exchange was normal. Though she never really understood why her parents divorced, she saw how happy they both were in their new marriages. When Dad and Mom did interact, they didn't fight with each other but had a mature, amicable relationship. Both parents had worked hard to make Lisa an important part of their new families, and Lisa loved both her stepparents. From all appearances, Lisa and her families had adjusted well to divorce.

During Lisa's senior year of college, her best friend, Kate, got engaged. As the maid of honor, Lisa poured over bridal magazines with Kate as they planned the big day. Walking back to her room one evening, Lisa began thinking ahead to her own wedding. As she wondered who would walk her down the aisle, she was dumbfounded by an overwhelming sadness that she couldn't explain. Eighteen years after the divorce, Lisa's sobs marked the first time she mourned her loss.

Triggers Defined

Lisa was experiencing what sociologist Judith Wallerstein calls the sleeper effect. Wallerstein explains the sleeper effect in her book *Second Chances: Men, Women and Children a Decade After Divorce* by telling Denise's story.

Denise had been the poster child for adjustment when Dr. Wallerstein last met with her at age fifteen. She made excellent grades, was musically gifted, showed no behavior problems, and was able to understand that her parents were not happy in their marriage. Dr. Wallerstein's only concern was Denise's tendency to hold her feelings in check. At age twenty-one, Denise announced that she was "into pain." She explained,

> All those years I denied feelings.... I lived with the absolute thought that I could live without love, without sorrow, without anger, without pain. That's how I coped with the unhappiness in my parents' marriage. And that's why I didn't get upset at the divorce. That's why I looked so good to you when I was little. Only that year, when I met Frank, did I become aware of how much feeling I was sitting on all those years.[1]

Dr. Wallerstein offers this insight into Denise's mind-set:

> [Her parents' divorce] produced in Denise deep-seated anxieties about relationships, fears that she banished to the farthest recesses of her mind. But the feelings endured, only to resurface ten years later. In a true sense, this can be considered a sleeper effect, a delayed reaction to an event that happened many years earlier.
> ...The sleeper effect primarily affects young women, in part because girls seem to fare much better psychologically immediately after divorce than boys. Because girls appear so much better

adjusted socially, academically and emotionally every step of the way after divorce, much of the research of the effects of divorce on children emphasizes the good recovery of girls compared with the more troublesome experience of boys.

As young men enter adulthood, their behavior is more congruent with their pasts, reflecting difficulties encountered throughout their high school years. Many girls may seem relatively well adjusted even through high school and then—wham! Just as they undertake the passage to adulthood and their own first serious relationships, they encounter the sleeper effect.[2]

While Wallerstein's sleeper effect is primarily set off by intimacy issues, additional triggers include situations, senses, and even songs. Marriage counselors Beverly and Tom Rodgers address this delayed response to divorce in their book *Adult Children of Divorced Parents: Making Your Marriage Work*. The couple, who each experienced parental divorce as children, explain the scientific basis for our overly emotive responses, especially as they relate to our marriages:

The brain stem...is the very primitive mammalian part of the human brain. It does not have the ability to take in information and observe human behavior. It can only react to the stimuli it receives.... It is the seat of very powerful emotions and is our self-defense monitor. It responds in a fight or flight manner when we are in real or perceived danger. There is something else that is very significant about the limbic system. It is atemporal, which means that it has no sense of time. Therefore, a memory at age five can be recalled at age twenty-five and bring up all the sensations or emotions that a person felt at the time of the original trauma....

Think for a moment about a time when you got really sick

on a certain type of food. Perhaps you got a violent case of food poisoning. Now think about that food. Do you feel a little nauseated as you recall this? That feeling of nausea is your old brain remembering the trauma you felt. We call this feeling an "old brainer"....

Old brainers aren't so difficult to deal with when it comes to food triggers or upset stomachs, but what if these old brainers are triggered in the marriage?... This was the case with Tom and I. We had vivid memories of our parents' divorces. These memories would haunt us early in our marriage. If we would get in a conflict, many of these fight or flight responses were activated. We had no idea what was happening to us. So many of our responses were overreactive, but we seemed not to be able to control them. We later realized that our old brains were being triggered, and we were experiencing reactivity [using more emotion in a situation than it deserves].[3]

Mike, whose parents divorced when he was two, illustrates this point. Abandoned by his father when he was a baby, Mike has a fierce sense of protection and respect for his mom. He acknowledges her sacrifice as she struggled to be both Mike's mom and dad. She never remarried, instead putting all her energy into creating a safe home for her son. As a young boy, Mike assumed the role of man of the house, taking care of maintenance chores and tending to his mom's emotional needs. Whenever situations would arise that typically involved a dad, Mike would launch into a vengeful diatribe about his own father being solely responsible for the divorce. In his mind, it was inconceivable that his mom could have done anything to contribute to the breakup.

As an adult, Mike struggled in his romantic relationships because he lacked a model of partnership and reconciliation. The first time a new girlfriend would let him down, it would trigger the pain of his father's abandonment, and this amplified his disappointment. As a result, he would walk away from the relationship, never realizing that, by default, he had become just like his dad.

Triggers are those emotional or situational events that lance the bubble of our self-protective devices. Unaware of their power, we are both overwhelmed and embarrassed by our emotive responses. Triggers elicit extreme emotions because the little boys and little girls inside us are crying out to have our most painful owies kissed and made better.

As children we had the subconscious ability to shut off our emotions when they overwhelmed us. Unless our parents were mindful of this tendency, or if as adults we are intentional about cleaning out our emotional closets, we risk living numb lives. We can't truly love without risking hurt. We can't truly find joy if we avoid the possibility of pain. When we continue to live in the safe emotional zone we've made for ourselves, we not only keep out all that we fear, but we gate away all that we desire as well.

Tupperware has for years sold the classic red and blue Shape-O toy. The circular object includes bright yellow handles that allow a child to pull it apart and dump out a bevy of different-shaped pieces. The toy provides a fitting illustration of how triggers affect us. As we go about our everyday business, we have within us all those pieces of emotion, but they are stuffed inside, away from our conscious thoughts. When we experience a trigger event, such as our wedding, our emotional gates are pulled apart like that toy, and all those pieces fall out. If we just walk away, we are left empty. If we remain, we must deal with the mess of the assorted pieces. To heal, we must do the hard work of fitting each shape into the appropriate slot. We do this by identifying our potential triggers and choosing our response to them.

When we can identify potential triggers, we decrease the likelihood of those events transporting us back to the emotional battlefield. As we explore a few common triggers, ask God to show you the triggers with the greatest capacity to set you off.

EMOTIONAL TRIGGERS

Emotional triggers hit us by means of subtle scenarios, leaving us bewildered by our emotional explosion. In the days prior to 9/11, one of my emotional triggers set off each time my plane landed. Couples kissing and families welcoming their loved ones home at the gate stirred in me an intense sorrow, because I wanted so much for someone to think I was such a priority that they would pay the parking fee just to meet me at the earliest possible moment. From a pragmatic perspective, I knew that meeting outside the baggage claim was more practical, but that trigger defined a moment I wanted to be sentimental.

Social events can also activate our triggers. Gatherings with friends can elicit that sinking feeling when the one we're meeting is late or aloof, and we must fight the feelings of abandonment and displaced priority.

As a generation intimately aware of divorce comes of age and overtakes the media, music and movies, even commercials, will increasingly include triggers, either because they name our unspoken sorrows or they share our yearning for what may never be. For years I could not listen to music from the late '80s because every song made me seventeen again, complete with all the tension and anguish that defined that year of my life.

Erin walked out of the movie *Hope Floats* in tears because watching the little girl's anguished screams as she stood in the dust left by her father's car ripped open a heart still hurting from her own father's painful parting fifteen years earlier. *Bye Bye Love, Kramer vs. Kramer,* and other movies centered on a divorce theme are painful triggers, but they can also help us access those childhood hurts so that we can finally process them as adults.

SITUATIONAL TRIGGERS

Situational triggers are those precipitated by events, including holidays. Theresa recounted the trigger of Christmas:

We flew (three little ones included) to Florida in hopes of spending quality time with my brother. Unfortunately, my dad lives too close. Don't get me wrong, we love my dad, but with it comes Dad's latest girlfriend. So Dad comes in, and within a day he has intruded enough on my brother and his family that my sister-in-law launches into a nasty fight with him. My dad wanted to leave his girlfriend with our kids for the day so the rest of us could hang out. They exchange a few harsh words and everyone pretends nothing happened. Dad scurries off to spend the night with his "other" girlfriend. The night is filled with tears and hurt feelings, and we all go to bed whispering to our spouses about what happened.

The next day (Christmas Eve) is spent with lots of alcohol to cover up the true feelings. Christmas comes and goes and everyone focuses on the kids so they don't have to talk with one another. The day after Christmas, my husband and I get on a plane to go home. We go straight to my in-laws' house for their Christmas. The next day we board another plane to Denver to see my mom and another brother and his family for Christmas.

It is exhausting emotionally and physically, and I never was able to spend any quality time with my brother in Florida. And I didn't get a chance to see my stepdad (my mom's second husband) and his family at all. Christmas brings back too many memories, memories of lots of fighting, lots of arguments, and lots of tears. It does not seem to be joyous for me. It makes me sad, and I want it to pass quickly. At the same time, when it does go, I feel sad for the loss. I'm not sure why…maybe the idea of all the memories never to come.

In addition to Christmas, other situational triggers include:
• weddings and baby showers

- getting stood up for a date or meeting
- a friend's engagement
- your birthday
- your parents' anti-anniversaries—the day of their separation and/or the day they officially divorced

TRANSITIONAL TRIGGERS

Transitional triggers surface as we approach new life stages.

At twenty-three, Gabe didn't think his parents' divorce two decades before had affected him. Priding himself on his independence and ability to adapt to change, he credited the divorce for teaching him those skills. Using humor to avoid the hard topics, he often joked that the divorce was a positive thing, "Hey! I get two Christmases, two birthdays…double presents for every occasion…what's not to like about that?" When a serious romance led to a visit with his girlfriend's parents, he found their obvious affection for each other unexpectedly unsettling. He explained, "All of a sudden, I felt utterly inadequate to be a husband or a father. I realized at that moment that I had no idea how to create what my girlfriend expected. My only goal for my own marriage was simply to avoid divorce."

For Brad Miles, of the group Everman, the transition to fatherhood forced him to face the underlying, unresolved issues with his dad. He shared with me:

> Two years ago my wife and I had a baby girl. I can't believe how
> crazy I am about her. In the months just before and after her birth,
> I was feeling the overwhelming love that a parent has for a child,
> and I became very angry that my relationship with my father had
> become so unimportant to him. I'm sure he would say that our
> relationship was important, but his actions clearly proved other-
> wise. He never fought to keep me as a major part of his life.

I remember when everything really came to a head. My brother returned from visiting him for a week one time when I was not able to be there. He was telling about all the fun things they did—going to Six Flags, playing Putt-Putt. Suddenly in the middle of his report he says, "Oh yeah, and Dad got married." He got married, and I had never met the woman, was not asked to be there, was not even called with the news. I found out from my brother. Suddenly all the things I suspected about how my father really felt about me were demonstrated right in front of my face. I saw firsthand right where I was on his list of priorities.

My mom had remarried as well in the meantime, and the man she married is an incredible man who I now call my dad. I remember going to youth choir practice that night very upset but trying to pretend like nothing was wrong. Suddenly I started bawling like a baby (not a cool thing for a sixth-grader to do). I wasn't even sure why I was crying at the time. I just knew I was upset. I half ran to the door, and as soon as I went out, my dad (the man my mother had married) was standing there. He knew I was upset, and he wanted to make sure that he was there when it all caught up with me. I realized then who my father was. I saw very plainly the difference between just being someone's biological father and being their dad. A dad desperately wants to wipe every tear. A dad thinks of his children before himself. Soon after that my father signed over parental rights, and my dad adopted me and my brother.

By the time my daughter was born, I honestly thought I had forgiven my father and had moved past any feelings of abandonment I may have had. But as I held my daughter for the first time, I was shaken to the core by the fact that my father did not love me the way I love my daughter. She is the entire world to me. I would give up everything I own or dream of being for a relationship with her. I just couldn't get over the fact that my father had made different choices.

Suddenly, I had self-esteem issues. I felt like the sixth-grader who had just realized his father didn't really value their relationship all over again. I felt exactly like I did that Sunday night when I went running out of the choir room.

Additional transitional triggers include:
- your engagement
- graduation and other milestone events
- your children's significant events
- the death of a parent

The Romance Trigger

As Wallerstein discovered, the prospect of initiating our own intimate relationships is the most universal trigger. Our fear that we may get divorced paralyzes us. Often at this point, we have a strong need to try to figure out *why* our parents divorced so that we can avoid their mistakes.

As we grow older, we will naturally compare our life to our parents' lives. Becky's mom was twenty when she married and thirty when she divorced, two children later. Though Becky actively dates now that she is in her twenties, she is utterly opposed to marriage before her thirtieth birthday. She wasn't even aware of the rule she had written for herself until a would-be fiancé pushed for the reason behind her snub. "I love Greg," she explained. "He is everything I want in a husband. But I know that Mom loved Dad when she was in her twenties too, so how do I know that this love will last into my thirties? I think maybe if I wait until I'm thirty to marry, then I'll be over whatever caused Mom to be unable to stay married to Dad."

When it comes to our own romantic relationships, we desperately want to know that we are choosing well. Because we have experienced the negative side of marriage, we are not anxious to enter the relationship thoughtlessly. In fact, our pasts may cause us to be so overly cautious, and our expectations so lofty, that not even Christ Himself could live up to our requirements.

In reality, people are imperfect and relationships are fluid. As much as we may want to control or accurately predict our future, the fact remains that the "we" of our relationship is like a boat drifting without a rudder. If we are not intentional about our course, we will not reach our destination. As people, we will have bad days, make wrong choices, and occasionally allow our emotions to overcome our reason. We must marry knowing that our spouse's imperfections are evidence only of his (or her) humanity, not proof of his (or her) incompatibility with us.

That said, here are a few questions to think about when considering marriage:

- Does my relationship with this person enhance or distract from my growing relationship with Christ? How do I affect this person's relationship with Christ?
- Are the life goals of this person compatible with the calling I feel God has placed on my life? Can I serve God better with or without this person?
- Do the things I like about this person form a strong enough foundation that the things I don't like are inconsequential in comparison?
- Have we worked through issues of money, sex, expectations, conflict resolution, spiritual interpretations, and the role of faith in our life and marriage?
- Have I worked through the issues stemming from my parents' divorce, and do we realize that issues will continue to arise? Do

we have a plan for anticipating and dealing with those issues in an honoring way?

- Can I honestly share my feelings and frustrations with this person, and can I support him or her without resentment—even when this person is the source of my hurt feelings or frustration?
- When we have disagreements, do we have enough unity that the disagreement is less a matter of him (or her) against me and more a matter of us against the conflict?
- When I think of this person as a potential parent, do I like what I see?
- Imagine that you have made the decision to marry this person. Don't tell anyone, but wear that emotion for a few days. How does it feel? Does it fill you with dread and fear, or peace and anticipation?[4]
- Am I willing to forsake *all* others (family, friends, members of the opposite sex) to make this person my first earthly priority? Am I willing to choose to love, honor, and seek this person's best interest, despite my feelings at any given time, and regardless of his or her willingness to do the same for me?
- Does our relationship have the support and approval of those closest to us?
- Are we both capable and willing to put the other's needs before our own wants?
- Are we both committed to a lifelong marriage, willing to work out our differences in a mutually satisfying manner?
- Is this person my best friend?
- Do I believe, and am I willing to accept, that this person is God's best for me?

If you can accurately and honestly answer in the affirmative to most of these questions, you have likely chosen well.

The Wedding Trigger

The culmination of the romance trigger is the wedding itself, because, though the ceremony is focused on the future, every little detail drips with symbolism and sentimentality. If the wedding presents a rare reunion of our divorced parents, the awkward air reminds family and friends of the fissure not far from everyone's mind.

While etiquette experts may have strong opinions of how to handle weddings with divorced parents, each divorce is different and needs to be considered in a way that respects your unique situation.

Please hear this: *It is OKAY to make the day your day.* This truth may go against every people-pleasing, go-between mediating, conflict-avoiding, coping mechanism you've ever acquired, so hear it again: It is OKAY to make the day your day. It is *okay* to consider your feelings, desires, opinions, and preferences before those of your parents. It takes great courage to marry in light of all the brutal reality you've seen, and yet some parents will make it harder by acting up, out, and indignant as they declare their demands on your day. Be respectful of your parents, but keep in mind that a successful marriage requires a transference in allegiance. The family you create with your spouse becomes your priority and opportunity to create the family you've idealized. Planning your wedding offers a wonderful opportunity to start that process of actualization. Romans 12:18 offers a wise counsel for this situation, "If it is possible, as far as it depends on you, live at peace with everyone."

Several factors can hinder your parents' ability to maturely participate and enjoy your day:

- the amount of time since the divorce
- the presence of new spouses and significant others
- the pressure of spending time together and money on a common goal

- their own perhaps-unexplored triggers as memories of their own marriage demand their emotional attention

When making your wedding arrangements, adjust your expectations for the reality of the situation. Gently remind your parents that you have had to adjust to their decision to divorce. You are simply asking them to return the favor for this one event. Your wedding is between you and your fiancé(e), not them.

The divorce-influenced decisions you'll have to make include the following:

Invitations

- How will you word your engagement and wedding announcements? Will you include all of your parents, or just the ones who had custody? What about stepparents?

The Guest List

- What will you do if you don't want one of your parents to attend? What feelings might crop up later if you don't offer that invitation?
- What do you do when one parent doesn't want the other to attend and makes threats to curry your favor? One newlywed reflected, "My father doesn't have a girlfriend, but my mother has a boyfriend. I have to live with that whether I like it or not, so I will invite both my parents and allow them each to bring a date. I am sure my mother will bring her boyfriend, but that is her prerogative. I am not inviting him; she is. It will be my day, but if she wants him there, she has that option. If they don't like it, that is not my problem... The divorce was not my idea."
- How will you handle stepparents and significant others—not only their presence, but also their roles? Will you include them on the program?

- How will you decide which of your parents' friends may attend? How will you deal with the discomfort of a recent divorce when guests are unsure how to talk to either parent without implying that they have chosen a side?

The Ceremony

- Who will give the bride away? This is often one of the most difficult decisions for a bride to make. There is nothing wrong with having both parents walk the bride down the aisle; in fact, it's the norm in Jewish weddings. Consider a creative approach that fits your situation. One bride offered, "I'm taking a historical approach: Dad and Mom will walk me part way, then my various stepparents will join the procession in order of how they joined the family until we get to the altar. When the pastor asks who is giving me away, they'll all say, 'We do!'"

Photos

- What will be your approach to photos? Do you want them to reflect your family as it currently is, or do you want to acknowledge all those who have contributed to your formation?
- Would your parents be willing to be in a picture together? How do you feel about stepparents and significant others participating? How about stepsiblings and half-siblings?

Planning the Wedding

- As more young couples plan weddings with the complication of divorced parents (and even divorced grandparents), the Internet will be a growing resource. Type "divorced parents wedding planning" in any search engine to discover the latest.
- Meet with your parents separately to discuss their initial thoughts and wishes, as well as to present your own thoughts, including

expectations and the role each parent will play. Determine what is negotiable to you and what is not. Be prepared to steer the discussion away from the other parent.

- Consider a special role for each parent.
- After engagement, consider writing a warm letter to your parents, incorporating the following points:
  - ▼ Express gratitude for their parts in shaping your development.
  - ▼ Invite them to participate in your wedding day.
  - ▼ Acknowledge that you understand the day may be difficult for them emotionally.
  - ▼ Request that they prepare themselves to put aside any hurts, bitterness, or any other emotion that might take away from the joy of your celebration and the comfort of your guests.
  - ▼ Assure them that you have put much thought into the significance of each detail. Explain anything that may seem unusual or hold the potential to be misinterpreted or misunderstood.
  - ▼ Outline your expectations for their behavior, roles, and participation in the ceremony. Expectations can include ultimatums, if necessary. Financial contributions should not be included as expectations.
  - ▼ List your requests and wish list of acts and interactions that you know may be more difficult for them. Plan your wedding as if none of these things will happen, and receive them as gifts if they do.

Once we have identified our triggers, we will be better able to respond appropriately to them by acknowledging the feelings evoked, recognizing our limitations, surrounding ourselves with safe people, adjusting our expectations, and determining our responses.

ACKNOWLEDGE OUR FEELINGS

No matter how seemingly insignificant the trigger, acknowledge the feelings it evokes. Remember that grief involves a process that comes and goes. As you become aware of losses that you need to grieve, give yourself permission to do so.

It really is okay to feel our feelings, even if there are decades between cause and effect. As we learn to acknowledge our feelings when we feel them, we increase the likelihood that our emotions and emotional level will appropriately match the situation. They will no longer be misplaced or misdirected. After some practice, it will become second nature. For the smaller issues, you may acknowledge your awareness with a simple shrug and think, *Oh, that's where that's coming from.*

RECOGNIZE OUR LIMITATIONS

Most of our triggers will involve situations in which at least one parent is unable or unwilling to fulfill a socially expected role because of the divorce. Acknowledging our limitations means realizing that we can't control how others respond. Sometimes it is simply not possible to make a decision that all the members in our disjointed family will like.

At that most difficult junction, we must make decisions that best enhance our ability to heal and enjoy healthy relationships. Planning primarily with our parents' preferences in mind, in the case of a wedding, is focusing on the past. So we choose to respond with honor, while moving forward to focus on our future family. In an ironic twist, we're now the ones making the hard choices, and we do so hoping that at some point our parents will be able to make peace with our decisions.

One young bride acknowledged her limitations in a letter to her mom, "Your divorce will be extremely real and near to me on my wedding day, and every day as I plan it. It'll be real when I decide who walks me down the aisle, knowing that no decision I make will be painless to everyone. It'll be on your mind as you think about your own wedding and wonder if my marriage will last. It'll be on Dad's mind as he sits with his wife, looking at me as he remembers marrying you."

SURROUND OURSELVES WITH SAFE PEOPLE

Emotions can present a frightening reality. As I have ventured to embrace my emotional side, I have realized that one of the coping mechanisms I adopted was to think my feelings, rather than experience them. Once I acknowledged this pattern, I became intentional in my efforts to be authentic with my feelings. Sometimes my expressions were messy, so I surrounded myself with those I could trust with these fledgling feelings.

The safe people who surrounded me have helped me recognize feelings I had suppressed, denied, or explained away. My accountability partner has been a gentle coach in this regard. I would describe my thoughts on something, and she would say, "Oh, you're mad," or "Jen, that's love, you know!"

An important component of anticipating our triggers is knowing ourselves well enough to tell those we trust what our triggers are and how they can best help us beat them. My close friends know that Christmas is hard because it marks the anniversary of my first family's failure. My birthday is difficult because I still struggle with the guilt of knowing Mom waited until my eighteenth to leave my stepdad.

My friends know that I battle the feeling of not being a priority to anyone, and they do their best to show me otherwise. Jen calls to check in on me when I seclude myself to lick my lingering wounds. Rach sends me cards with just the truth I need to hear. Melissa leaves such silly messages on my answering machine that I can't help but laugh. Ang travels across the state to be a part of our parties. In their enthusiastic gushes of love, they are washing away years of feeling unwanted.

While we may bristle at this level of vulnerability, we cannot expect others to read our minds or know our needs. We must take the initiative. Once we ask, our safe people can:

- help us identify our emotions
- share evidence of growth they see
- remind us of the truth when our thoughts and emotions are mired in the lie
- give us permission to explore our past, grieve, and talk about our hurts and healing
- welcome us into their homes when ours seems foreign
- draw us out when depression, sadness, and loneliness overwhelm us
- protect us by serving as our advocates and/or buffers when needed (This may prove especially helpful when planning a wedding)
- love us without condition

Adjust Our Expectations

The residual effects of divorce lessen in intensity as we learn to anticipate our triggers, but we may never come to a point where they are fully alleviated. Acknowledging this reality will help us deal with it better. Mom and Dad might never be willing to be nice to each other. Mom might never say she's sorry for hurting us. Dad might never be willing to be a consistent part of our life. It stinks and it hurts, but these limitations are beyond our control. Time, distance, maturity, and a greater reliance on God as the Father of our family and source of our identity will soften the impact of future blows, but we should not be surprised if our sadness lingers throughout our lifetime.

With this knowledge, our goal is no longer to reach a point where we no longer hurt, but rather to accept our scars. In doing so, we can adjust our expectations accordingly and determine responses that help us grow into spiritually and emotionally healthy persons.

DETERMINE OUR RESPONSE

Throughout this book, we examined different ways our family has affected our life. Given our reflection and the example modeled to us through Christ, we have the ability to determine our response.

Mike stated the process succinctly when he wrote:

> Being a child of divorce and a Christian gives me so much motivation to break the habits that my parents passed on. I believe in a few key things:
>
> 1. Moving away from the family and creating my own family in my community was the best thing I ever did. My friends here are more than a family to me.
>
> 2. I need to rely on Jesus and His Word to fill my head…not the negative screwed up thoughts my parents put into my head.
>
> 3. Jesus has the power to break the strongholds and bad habits left over from my family.
>
> I can say that being a child of divorce makes me so motivated to communicate with my spouse and make our relationship a top priority. The day my dad told me he and my mom were separated is more vivid in my mind than any other day of my life. It puts a lump in my throat even as I write this. That was *eighteen years ago!* I never want my children to go through that. At the time, I don't think I had any clue what I was feeling, but when I look back I

can't believe how painful it was. I fear being like them…I fear making the same mistakes…I fear screwing up my children's lives. At the same time, Christ is there to set me free from fear. And THAT is the key to breaking the strongholds left over from my family.

We have talked a lot about the triggers of romantic relationships and our wedding in this chapter. Now let's focus on the marriage itself. In the next chapter, we'll examine how to create a new marriage model.

Word

Therefore, prepare your minds for action; be self-controlled; set your hope fully on the grace to be given you when Jesus Christ is revealed. (1 Peter 1:13)

Reflection

- Think of the divorce and how it has affected your life and acknowledge all the feelings that come to mind using "I" statements, such as, "I felt abandoned when Dad left."
- Visualize the life you desire. Have your responses to triggers, in general, enhanced or hindered your likelihood of creating that life?
- What are some of the limitations you face because of the divorce?
- Who are your safe people? What do they need to know to help you diffuse your triggers? Do they know this information?
- List some of the emotional triggers you have experienced. What caused them, and what were your responses?
- What situational triggers do you anticipate experiencing in the future? Determine your response now.

Challenge

Think of your next likely trigger. Write out your plan of action using the process outlined in this chapter. If appropriate, discuss it with your parents.

Read

Adult Children of Divorce: Making Your Marriage Work by Beverly Rodgers and Tom Rodgers (Resource Publications, 2002)

Second Chances: Men, Women and Children a Decade After Divorce by Judith S. Wallerstein and Sandra Blakeslee (Houghton Mifflin, 1989)

Create Our Own Marriage Model

Effect: *The experience of divorce distorts our expectations of marriage.*

Hope: *We can choose to create a new, more realistic model of what marriage can be.*

Lifelong marriages are not created through happenstance. They are the result of constant attention and hard work. Yet, as children of divorce, we don't have an accurate picture of a good marriage to guide us. Even if our parents have happily remarried, the picture is still a bit blurred because we don't want it to take two tries to get it right.

Many of us are so focused on what we don't want—divorce—that we fail to consider what we need. A woman says, "Dad was so vocal about everything, so I'm going to find a man who never yells." As a result, she may find someone who doesn't express his emotions at all. She'd be better off to look for someone who can verbalize his emotions in a healthy way, who can express his preferences without putting down her own.

Our confidence in marriage is already tentative. The last thing we need to be reminded of is the possibility of failure. I don't have to tell you that despite our desperate desires it's possible we may end up divorced ourselves. You wouldn't be reading this book if you weren't keenly aware of this potential. My objective here is not to put even more fear in your heart but rather to give you hope.

As a single person, I knew that to research this chapter, it was vitally important that I focus on the positive. It's too easy to proceed by opposites. I wanted to help you—and me—develop a clear, accurate picture of a good marriage. To do that, I had in-depth conversations with several Christian couples who have been married only to each other for at least thirty years. I wanted to know how they had managed to stay married and what advice they might have for those of us who want healthy, lasting marriages. Much of their wisdom and insight has been woven into the fabric of this book, but the models and mentors I met shaped this chapter in particular.

Here is a summary of their advice on how to have a lifelong marriage:
- Confront shadow beliefs about marriage.
- Establish safeguards to protect your marriage.
- Take advantage of resources.
- Accept the spiritual reality of marriage.
- Elevate the "we."
- Pursue mutually defined goals.
- Deal with conflict constructively.
- Celebrate marriage milestones.

Let's take a closer look at each of these recommendations.

Confront Shadow Beliefs

Shadow beliefs are ideas that we have accepted as truth without conscious consideration, when in reality, those thoughts are either lies or myths. Let's look at some shadow beliefs.

Shadow Belief: Of course I'll get married!
Reality: Marriage is not a given.

Children of divorce often desire marriage for closure to the past. While it's natural for us to want to be married, none of us can assume that God's plan for us includes a partner. We could spend our whole lives preparing for marriage and yet never marry. For that reason, it's far more productive for singles to focus on becoming healthy and whole—which is what God desires for each of us—than on fretting about how to avoid divorce.

If we are misplacing our hopes for happiness on a husband (or wife), we need to confess our idolatry. If we desire marriage, we can ask God to give us this gift, but at the same time we must make our request with an open, undemanding hand. God knows our past, our present, and our future. He loves us beyond what we can imagine and promises to bring good out of all that we have experienced if we let Him.

Bebo Norman is a popular songwriter in Christian music circles because his poetic lyrics touch the single soul. When I interviewed him about his third album, he shared with me a recent revelation about longing. He said that so much of our lives are spent trying to fulfill our longings, when in reality, God gave us those longings to remind us of our separation from Him. They offer us an opportunity to thank God for the promise of our true homecoming. If ever we reach a point where we no longer feel that tug of want, we have fully denied the reason for our existence.[1]

If you are single, it may ultimately be God's will for you to marry, but for today you are single, so for today seek your satisfaction in that state.

Shadow Belief: If I marry the right person, marriage will be easy.
Reality: Even the best marriages have periods of struggle.

According to the movies and magazines that clutter the media landscape, if we just find and fall in love with the right person, our life will be forever rosy and we'll live happily ever after. If we believe this fantasy, then as soon as we encounter challenges in our marriages—and we will—we assume that we married the "wrong" person. While it's true that some people will make better marriage partners for us than others, there is no such thing as the "right" person.

In reality, marriage is a partnership between two imperfect people, and it's a gamble, because we cannot anticipate what twists and bends the road of life might take. We also take the risk that our partner may not be all we perceive him or her to be, and our partner assumes that same risk with us. Some seasons will be hard, no question, but the difficulty or the duration does not mean divorce is our destiny.

One couple, married thirty-four years, shared their surprise at the challenges children brought to their marriage. Sleepless nights filled with constant crying, monotonous days dictated by the demands of young children, date-night and getaway budgets squeezed to make room for diapers and doctor bills all took their toll. After one especially trying day, they committed to a nightly snuggling ritual, where they prayed for their partnership, assured each other that the season would pass, affirmed their commitment to maintain their marriage, and dreamed together of how satisfying it would be when they sent their children off into the world from a stable home.

With all the complaining and caricatures of spouses, one might think we approach marriage at gunpoint. Yet, in our culture, we choose our spouses. We esteem love as the seal of our deal, and yet when the feelings fade, we question our selection. It's easier on our egos to find fault outside our own lack of commitment, but statistics clearly show that marriages die not because love dies, but because our decision to love does.

Shadow Belief: If I marry a Christian, our faith will insure us against divorce.
Reality: Statistics show that Christians divorce at the same rate as non-Christians.

Although our faith gives us access to the skills and commitment needed to make a marriage successful, don't make the mistake of thinking that

God is some sort of genie who will protect you from the normal struggles and realities of married life. Instead, take steps that will increase the likelihood that you will enjoy a marriage without divorce.

Unfortunately, Amber and Justin learned this lesson too late. Amber relates:

Both my husband and I came from broken homes. We dated for four years before getting married. We took our faith as seriously as our desire to avoid divorce. We started off so strong and so intentionally. We were involved in Bible study, we read relationship books together, we served in our church together. We were the couple that everyone looked to as a model.

But after the kids came and time went on, we relaxed our efforts, and I think, in hindsight, took our marriage for granted. At least I did once I realized I had been married longer than my mom. Because of my husband's job, we moved around a lot. After a while, we stopped making church attendance a priority. Without a focused commitment to God—something above ourselves—we reverted to looking out for our own needs first. We became dissatisfied and instead of talking about it, we let it fester.

He became a workaholic, and I found solace in the arms of his best friend. It's been seven years since our divorce, and I wish I could just go back. I'm so ashamed of what I did. And worse, we both became what we tried so hard to overcome. I am a single mom, just like my mom. He is the estranged dad, just like his father.

Shadow Belief: Once in love, always in love.
Reality: Feelings fluctuate in intensity over time.

The state of our marital satisfaction is not static. Like our moods, it fluctuates depending on our circumstances, but those who work through their dissatisfactions now tend to have the most satisfactory relationships later. Linda Waite, coauthor of *The Case for Marriage,* discovered overwhelming confirmation of this reality. As part of her National Survey of Families and Households, couples were asked to rate their marriages on a scale from one to seven, one being very unhappy, seven being very happy. Those who rated their marriages a "one" had incredible turnarounds just five years later—if they stayed together. In fact, 77 percent of those who gave their marriage a very unhappy "one" rated their marriages either "very happy" or "quite happy" at the five-year follow-up.[2]

Every relationship ebbs and flows. If the tide didn't recede, we wouldn't be able to discover the treasures left behind. We can understand this concept in other areas of life, but it seems unromantic to accept it in our marriage. When we have to work hard for a goal, our satisfaction is much sweeter than when something is given to us without effort.

Shadow Belief: My spouse can (and should) meet all my needs.
Reality: If we are not whole before marriage, we will not be whole in marriage.

Only Christ completes us. Contrary to our desires or hopes, marriage does not fill the void of our longing or complete the closure of our childhood hurts. Our happiness may depend on our happenings, but joy, like fulfillment and love, comes from letting our feelings follow, not dictate, our choices.

ESTABLISH SAFEGUARDS

Understand How Divorce Happens
As believers, divorce presents a unique challenge. We are all sinners, but some sins are more complicated than others. Suppose I lie to a friend by

saying I did something that in actuality I failed to do. I can easily go to that friend, admit my wrongdoing, seek forgiveness, and rectify that situation. Case closed.

By comparison, divorce is the culmination of a series of ongoing choices to walk away from God's will:

- indulging the initial thought that divorce would be better than reconciliation
- deciding to entertain the fantasy that life would be better with someone else
- desiring to separate from my spouse
- rationalizing that perhaps God has made special consideration to release me from my marriage
- seeking others to confirm the decision my heart has made
- leaving the family home
- meeting with the divorce lawyer
- giving in to the temptation to exaggerate the difficulties to earn a more generous settlement
- deciding to sign those papers
- asserting that it is my right to remarry
- believing that God's ultimate desire for me is to be happy

At each step, the disillusioned spouse (or couple) has the option to seek reconciliation, but each decision on the road to divorce hardens the heart and diminishes the ability to make that choice. Divorce, by definition, requires one to adopt a theology in which the supreme god is self-satisfaction.

Knowing that the decision to divorce is rarely a spontaneous one, couples can consider the steps above as a series of flags in increasingly flamboyant shades of red. We can establish safeguards by discussing together how to proactively prevent each step. One of the husbands I interviewed shared how crassly his coworkers talked about their wives. As a young husband, he was horrified to see these men show signs of infidelity. So, early in their marriage, he and his wife established a rule that in an attempt to weed out seeds of discontent, they would avoid saying anything negative about each other to other people.

Make Divorce More Difficult

When I was growing up, one of my relatives wore a shirt that said, "My next husband will be rich." I hated that shirt. I cringed at the casual approach to commitment it implied and the disposition toward divorce it displayed.

Divorce is not something that should be taken lightly or made fun of. We need to be vigilant against allowing even the thought of divorce as a solution to our struggles.

We can do this by inviting accountability so that others can help us honor our vows. One couple I know had a copy of their vows framed before their wedding. At the reception, they invited guests to sign their names around the matting as a promise to hold the couple to their commitment. The frame is hung in the couple's living room to show all who enter that their partnership is permanent.

My accountability partner is a newlywed. One of the ways I help her to honor her vows is to ask her each week to tell me three new things she has discovered to appreciate about her husband. Because she knows I will ask, she has developed a mind-set of looking at her husband with appreciative eyes.

Take Advantage of Resources

Attend Marriage Conferences

In addition to spending time together away from the kids and the responsibilities of home, all six of the happily married couples I interviewed enthusiastically endorsed the benefit of annual marriage conferences. Taking time to attend these seminars demonstrates to our spouse our commitment to the ongoing improvement of our marriage and provides the opportunity to tweak the patterns set by the tyranny of the urgent. In addition to national conferences like FamilyLife's "I Still Do" or Tommy Nelson's "Song of Solomon" seminars, check out what the churches in your area have to offer. For a more intimate experience, I've included a marriage retreat itinerary in Appendix C.

Read Good Books on Marriage

When I read *Sacred Marriage* by Gary Thomas with its underlying premise, "What if the purpose of marriage is to make us holy more than to make us happy?" I understood for the first time the intended parallel between a husband and wife's love for each other and God's love for His bride, the church. I realized that marriage could be a spiritual discipline, an opportunity for us to love God in a tangible way by loving our spouse. Viewing marriage in this new way gave me confidence in my ability to be successful at marriage. Because I could see consistency in my commitment to Christ, even when it was hard, even when I didn't feel like being faithful, I found hope that I could be equally committed to my spouse in marriage. As Thomas puts it:

> In a man-centered view, we will maintain our marriage as long as
> our earthly comforts, desires and expectations are met. In a God-
> centered view, we preserve our marriage because it brings glory to
> God and points a sinful world to a reconciling Creator.[3]

Such a high view of marriage is a challenging one for adult children of divorce, yet it offers an odd comfort in that it addresses our desire for stability and acknowledgment of reconciliation lost:

> The last picture I want to give the world is that I have decided to
> stop loving someone and that I refuse to serve this person anymore

or that I have failed to fulfill a promise I made many years before. Yet this is precisely the message many Christians are proclaiming through their actions.... We can't carry a message well if we don't live it first. How can I tell my children that God's promise of reconciliation is secure when they see that my own promises don't mean a thing? They *may* get over it, but in that case I will have presented a roadblock rather than a stepping-stone to the gospel.... How can I proclaim reconciliation when I seek dissolution?[4]

I've listed several good books on marriage at the back of this chapter. Use this as a start, but then add to it by talking with successful couples you know. We need to put a face on our theories.

Find Mentors
Some churches match engaged couples with mentors to walk with them through the first year of marriage. I can't imagine a more meaningful way of engaging children of divorce with our church families. Even if your church doesn't currently provide this kind of program, you can take the initiative to learn from couples you respect. It may be helpful to seek out couples in a variety of life stages: newlyweds, new parents, survivors of the seven-year itch, empty nesters, grandparents, etc.

As you begin your mentoring relationships, the following questions may help break the ice:

1. What do you think it takes to have a successful marriage?
2. What was the most difficult time in your marriage? How did you get through it?
3. Did you ever consider divorce? What made you decide to stay together?
4. How do you define love?
5. What rules or habits have you developed to strengthen or govern your marriage?

6. How do you show love to your spouse when you don't feel love for him/her?
7. What do you most admire about your spouse?
8. How do you demonstrate to your spouse that you are trustworthy?
9. What has been the best means of conflict resolution in your marriage?
10. Was there anything you intentionally wanted to change within your marriage? How did you go about it?
11. How has your faith affected your marriage?
12. When you struggled with your marriage, who did you turn to, and what advice did you receive?
13. What do you like best about being married?

ACCEPT THE SPIRITUAL REALITY OF MARRIAGE

Despite our culture's somewhat successful attempt to make marriage an individualized decision, God created marriage to be a covenant—a three-way partnership of which He is a vital part. Therefore, there is a spiritual element to the relationship that may be debated, but it cannot be denied.

God wasted little time after the creation of Adam and Eve to institute the mystery of marriage: "Therefore shall a man leave his father and his mother, and shall cleave unto his wife: and they shall be one flesh" (Genesis 2:24, KJV).

The word *cleave* means "to stick, adhere, or cling to." Another definition is "to remain faithful." Remember the analogy of gluing two pieces of wood together? When we cleave to our spouse, there is no way to separate without losing part of ourselves in the process.

In one of the best books on the topic, *Covenant Marriage,* Fred Lowery wrote,

God designed marriage as a covenant relationship patterned after his covenant with Israel and Christ's covenant with his bride, the church.... America is a contract-oriented society. We like contracts because they allow us to bail out of a business deal or a relationship if things turn sour. Well, it may be fine to live by contract, but we must love by covenant.... Covenant is the way God has chosen to work in our lives and operate his kingdom. It is by covenant, and only by covenant, that you and I are found worthy to be a part of God's eternal kingdom. And it is by divine design that life's two most intimate and sacred relationships—the one with our heavenly Father and the one with an earthly spouse—are entered into and maintained on the basis of covenant. Covenant is the skeleton on which marriage is fleshed out. It is unbreakable.[5]

When we see our marriages as permanent rather than returnable, we apply more diligence in working out our issues.

Elevate the "We"

On our wedding day, we create a new entity—the "we." The "we" is the epitome of all our mutual goals and hopes and aspirations. With a little work, our "we" is our shared personality and person: who the two of us are together as a couple. We elevate the "we" when we train ourselves to think of our "we" as the preferred person in our marriage, whose health and growth we mutually decide to nurture above our own.

I like the way Fred Stoeker describes this "oneness" in *Every Woman's Desire:*

Envision the groom as a solid red candy cane, and the bride as a solid white candy cane. Through marriage, these two canes become woven into a single candy cane. The colors of both the husband

and wife, though distinct, now intertwine and are expressed together.[6]

In *God Will Make a Way*, John Townsend explains what it means to elevate the "we" in marriage:

> I think the key to a good marriage is this: being *in the marriage*— being totally invested, with all the parts of yourself, in building and sustaining the union. A married couple should love each other the same way that we are to love God: with all our heart, soul, mind, and strength (Mark 12:30). People who are truly in the marriage, people who are connecting every part possible to their mates—their good parts, bad parts, angry parts, loving parts, weak parts, and strong parts—have the best foundation for a lifetime of relationship.
>
> I'm not talking about being committed to marriage. Being in the marriage is more than being committed. Commitment has to do with agreeing to and fulfilling a covenant to one's spouse, and that is a good and necessary part of marriage. Some marriages, however, have high commitment but low connection. The covenant stands, but the hearts are not truly attached at the deepest levels. These couples will often have a stable and long-lasting relationship, but sometimes one or both individuals feels empty inside. The opposite problem also exists. Some have hearts that are genuinely bonded, but their commitment is weak. These couples do very well in good times, but fare poorly when things get rocky. Being in the marriage means being deeply committed and deeply connected at every juncture of one's self and one's life.[7]

In the twenty-five years since my mom and dad divorced, the one compliment my mom has consistently paid my dad is that he was great dancer. It struck me as odd that of all the character qualities my dad possesses, it is his prowess on the dance floor that my mom remembers in delight. In an effort to interact with my dad as an adult, I recently accepted his invitation to join him on a cruise to the Caribbean, my mom's favorite vacation destination. When I told her of the trip, she said, "Make sure he dances with you. He's such a wonderful dancer."

My dad and I didn't have the opportunity to dance. Not being especially graceful myself, however, my curiosity did lead me to observe the ballroom dance class in the upper deck lounge. Listening to the instructor explain the give and take of the tango, I realized that perhaps Mom loved dancing with Dad because it was the only time they learned to consider the other fully. Creating the fluid rhythm and rhyme of partnered poetry requires the ability to read your partner's flow and anticipate his or her next move. Each of our steps is intentionally placed in relation to our partner's. In dancing, two "I's" create a beautiful "we." In the dance of romance, couples waltz and whirl to the harmonious melody of their "we."

PURSUE MUTUALLY DEFINED GOALS

In earlier chapters we talked about the importance of knowing ourselves well and of being able to articulate our values and our goals. If you know yourself and what you want in the future, you will be more likely to marry someone who shares those values and goals.

If you are already married, you might consider creating a family constitution that outlines the goals and ground rules you and your spouse want to establish for your family. Post this constitution in a prominent place so that everyone in your family can refer to it easily.

Your family constitution might:
• outline shared values
• set rules for conflict resolution

- define what is and is not acceptable behavior
- set perimeters that protect your priorities

Some points may be based on the patterns of your past. For example, if infidelity or inappropriate relationships were part of your parents' problems, you might create a rule that no member of the opposite sex enters the house if your spouse isn't home.

The following sample of a family commitment models one written by Dr. Todd E. Linaman of the ministry Family Life Matters:[8]

Our Family Will…

1. Live our lives according to what we value and believe…even when it isn't popular. (See Joshua 24:15.)

2. Respond to one another with kind words and actions…even when we have been hurt or are angry! (See Ephesians 4:32 and Proverbs 14:29.)

3. Love all family members for who God created them to be…even when we don't understand our differences! (See 1 Peter 1:22.)

4. Understand one another before trying to be understood… even when we believe we are right! (See James 1:19.)

5. Make our home a place where everyone wants to be…even when we know it still won't be perfect! (See 1 Peter 4:8-9.)

6. Say "I love you" to one another every day…even when we don't feel like it! (See Proverbs 12:25 and 25:11.)

7. Admit when we are wrong and be quick to apologize…even when saying "I'm sorry" is difficult! (See Matthew 5:23-24.)

8. Spend time together having fun…even when there is work to be done! (See Matthew 6:34.)

9. Never give up on one another…even when the circumstances appear hopeless! (See Galatians 6:9-10.)

10. Forgive each other when we have been hurt or offended…even when forgiveness has not been asked for! (See Colossians 3:13.)

Deal with Conflict Constructively

We've seen conflict lead to separation and divorce, so it's quite common for us to avoid conflict at all costs. However, a fight doesn't have to mean the end of a relationship. In fact, contrary to our experience, conflict can build our character, improve our communication, and solidify our commitment. Conflict is inevitable in any relationship, and if handled appropriately, it can lead to restoration rather than separation. Rather than retreating or repressing our desires, we can view conflict as an opportunity to serve the other.

Consider these steps to turn conflict from a gut-tightening dread to a relationship-enhancing experience.

1. *Stop.* If a disagreement escalates into an emotional discussion, stop to pray. The shift in perspective will help you to focus on facts, not feelings. Ask God to help you view the conflict not as between you and your spouse, but between the two of you and the conflict itself.

2. *Agree.* Before moving on, confirm that the ultimate goal is to find a mutually workable solution that most enhances your "we." This puts the two of you on the same side.

3. *Assert.* Affirm your commitment to your marriage and love for each other. Acknowledge that conflict can bring about greater intimacy when the two of you resolve this issue.

4. *Establish.* Set ground rules before moving into discussion. Preferably, agree on rules before the discussion comes up. You may even want to post your rules of engagement around the house so that everyone will learn to fight fairly. A few suggestions:

   - In essentials, unity; in nonessentials, liberty; in everything, love—St. Augustine.[9]

- Don't bring up past or additional issues.
- Don't make things worse by saying things you can't take back.
- Avoid blanket statements ("You never"; "I always").
- Use language that shows ownership of your own actions ("I won't" versus "I can't"; "I will" versus "I'll try"; "Would you" versus "You should").
- Focus on resolving the issue rather that attacking the person.

5. *Assume.* Assume the best in the other person. As Goethe wrote, "Treat people as if they were what they ought to be, and you help them to become what they are capable of being."

6. *Listen.* Ask the other person to share his or her perspective. Listen attentively, without interruption. Attempt to understand what the person is trying to convey without responding to that information.

7. *Affirm.* Show that you have listened well by repeating the other person's concern from his or her perspective.

8. *Explain.* Present your perspective without exaggeration, emotional excess, or blame.

9. *Own.* Take ownership of your feelings and actions. Use "I" statements—"I feel X when you do Y because of Z. I'd prefer..."

10. *Consider:*
- Does the Bible address this issue specifically or in principle? If so, agree to submit to God's Word.
- What are our areas of agreement?
- Is there a choice that will better please Christ?
- Is either choice disrespectful or dishonorable to one of us?
- What is more important to me: being right or restoring unity?

- Issues of submission. Is either willing to concede (that is, a husband submits to his wife for the sake of oneness and demonstrating Christlike love, or a wife submits to her husband out of respect for his leadership)?

11. *Seek.* Pursue a compromise that honors both sides. Be willing to compromise on items that don't conflict with your convictions. If compromise is not possible, make a list of pros and cons, pray about it, take a break from it, or consider the issues of mutual submission.

12. *Decide.* Based on the factors above, decide to decide. You may need to take time apart to pray individually. If so, agree to return to the issue at a specific time, committed to come to a mutually agreeable conclusion. It may come down to one person submitting to the other for the sake of unity in the relationship. If you submit, you forfeit the right to hold resentment for that choice.

CELEBRATE MARRIAGE MILESTONES

Perhaps like me, you took your parents' anniversaries for granted until the day that day was no longer memorable. If you are married (or when you marry), celebrate your marriage milestones and invite your families to share them with you. Plant a tree, take a family portrait, watch your wedding video, tell your kids the story of your courtship, re-create your first date, reenact your proposal or enjoy a weekend getaway. Or do something similar to what a friend of mine, who is a talented seamstress, is doing. She designs a quilt square for each year of her marriage with images that depict the year's events. Celebrate the important moments—the day you met, your first date, the day you were engaged, and your wedding anniversary—with your family. Celebrate with your children, and in doing so, develop for them a positive picture of the miracle of marriage.

CREATE A COLLECTION OF MARRIAGE AND FAMILY SNAPSHOTS

Somewhere within each of us, we have pictures of what our ideal marriage and family looks like, even if we haven't seen it in tangible form yet. Whether we are married or single, our snapshots provide glimpses of our goals, and we've collected these images, knowingly or not, as we looked with longing at the intact families of our friends.

This chapter offers a lot of suggestions for how to create a lifelong marriage. I was intentional about displaying this assortment of snapshots because when it comes to our own romantic relationships, we are often unable to define what we want until we see an example of it. Not everything in this chapter may appeal to you, but I hope the variety of ideas will help you create an album of snapshots that is meaningful and vivid for you.

In my own photo album of family snapshots, for instance, I see a home where all the neighborhood kids want to hang out at our place, not because our rec room is full of the latest toys, but because our hearts are full of love. I want each person to know that he or she is a priority to me, and I want each one to hear me say "I love you" in some way every day. I want my husband and me to renew our vows after every disagreement and in front of our children on every anniversary. I want a hallway lined with family portraits taken each year, and a lifetime of entries written in our own journal.

My gallery of snapshots includes specific rituals as well. I want to be so affectionate with my husband that even though it embarrasses our kids, there will be no doubt about the depth of our love. I want a standing rule that there'll be "no leavin' without some lovin'," and we'll always greet each other with a kiss when we meet again. I want special occasions to really be special. I want my husband to treat our daughter like a princess on Valentine's Day, complete with roses and cards and kisses and promises that he'll never leave me or forsake me. I want her to *know* she'll never experience what Mommy did. I want birthdays to be celebrations of that person's life, and all day long I want to make that person a priority. And I want to always prepare an extra setting at our holiday gatherings because I know there is always someone who needs a place to go.

I have many more pictures in my album, but I share these examples to help you clearly see how to be specific in visualizing the family you want to create. If you're single, begin the process of collecting and creating marriage snapshots. What do you want your marriage and family to look like? What are your hopes and goals? Be specific as you write them down so you can refer to them later as you talk with a potential spouse to see if that person desires the same things. If you're married, be intentional about the habits you're forming and set up safeguards to strengthen and protect the marriage you and your spouse want to create.

As we approach our own marriages, it's vital that we be future-oriented and learn to articulate our hopes and goals. If we want our marriages to last a lifetime, we must be intentional about creating one that can survive the ebbs and flows of life. And most of all, we must passionately commit to choose to love.

Word

Unless the LORD builds the house, its builders labor in vain.
(Psalm 127:1)

Reflect

- Can you think of a couple that has a marriage like one you'd like to create for yourself? Describe it. Why do you think it works?
- What shadow beliefs have you accepted regarding marriage? Contrast them now with reality.

- What postdivorce traditions would you like to continue, and which new traditions do you want to incorporate?
- What elements would you include in a family constitution?
- If you are married, what partner in your marriage is most prominent: you, your spouse, or your "we"?
- What shared values are you (and your spouse) working to demonstrate in your marriage?
- What ground rules protect your priorities?
- Describe a disagreement you had with a parent, spouse, or friend. Then revisit the scenario, walking through the steps of conflict resolution (see pages 174–176). Include the dialogue of how the conversation might ideally go. Recognizing that you can't change the other person's perspective, how could you alter your response to the situation in the future?
- What are some of your marriage and family snapshots?

Challenge

If you are married, set aside a weekend for your own marriage retreat. If you are single, spend some time prayerfully considering the guidelines in this chapter as you create a collection of marriage snapshots.

Read

The Covenant Marriage by Fred Lowery (Howard, 2002)

Every Woman's Desire by Fred Stoeker and Stephen Arterburn (WaterBrook, 2001)

His Needs, Her Needs by Willard Harley (Revell, 2001)

How to Act Right When Your Spouse Acts Wrong by Leslie Vernick (WaterBrook, 2001)

The Most Important Year in a Woman's Life, The Most Important Year in a Man's Life by Robert and Bobbie Wolgemuth and Mark and Susan DeVries (Zondervan, 2003)

Passages of Marriage by Frank and Mary Alice Minirth, Brian
and Deborah Newman, and Robert and Susan Hemfelt
(Nelson, 1991)

Sacred Marriage by Gary Thomas (Zondervan, 2000)

*Unclaimed Baggage: Dealing with the Past on Your Way to a Stronger
Marriage* by Don and Jan Frank (NavPress, 2003)

What Children Learn from Their Parents' Marriage by Judith Siegel
(Quill, 2000)

Choose to Love

Effect: *The experience of divorce distorts our understanding of love and commitment.*

Hope: *We can choose to love well.*

The phrase *I love you* holds incredible power. How closely we have
guarded those three little words!

Lauren's parents divorced when she was thirteen, and she dreaded the
prospect of telling her boyfriend that she loved him. Even though she and
Brian had grown up together in the same small town and had dated
steadily all through high school, those three little words struck fear in her
heart. She did not want to say them unless she was confident that she
meant them to be permanent. She told me:

> Brian and I dated a long time before I thought about saying "I
> love you," and even when I thought about it, I struggled with the
> idea. It was something my heart felt, but my mind didn't want to
> allow those words to come out. Through many discussions I
> decided that it was all right to say those words if that was how I
> felt for him. I felt love for him and there was nothing wrong with
> saying that. God has commanded us to love one another. I loved
> my friends and family. The friendship I had created with Brian
> allowed me to love him. Telling him I loved him didn't mean I
> wanted to marry him... It meant I loved him. I didn't have to
> regret those feelings or those words if we didn't get married,

because I truly felt love for him and there was freedom in expressing that feeling.

Growing up with divorce, we learned that when it comes to love, we should grab what we can, when we can, for as long as we can. What Lauren was able to recognize is that her love for Brian was not validated because he reciprocated it. Instead, her love was valid because it was the honest acknowledgment of her loving actions toward him.

While Lauren was afraid she might have to retract her words, others of us are afraid to be open to love. In his book *Inside Out,* Larry Crabb offers this insight into our fear of vulnerability: "The sins of fathers are passed on to children, often through the dynamic of self-protection. It hurts to be neglected, and it creates questions about our value to others. So to avoid feeling the sting of further rejection, we refuse to give that part of ourselves we fear might once again be received with indifference."[1]

Many children of divorce identify strongly with that statement. In fact, when I asked several adult children of divorce about their ability to form healthy, intimate relationships and their desire for marriage, they responded with one of the following:

- "I value my independence."
- "I like doing things on my own. It's just the way I am."
- "I don't think my parents' divorce affected me. I'm just not in any hurry to get married myself."

In addition, almost every answer included the emphatic phrase, *"I will not get divorced."*

Fear lurks behind most of these statements and often keeps us from the love we want. As children of divorce, we fear marriage because we fear divorce, but before we even venture that far, we fear love because we fear failure, betrayal, and the possibility of abandonment. We fear risk because we don't want to revisit the intense pain of rejection again. We fear others because they might not deem us worthy of love, and we fear that we might not be capable of committed love. We fear marriage and parenthood because we fear being responsible for making our own children feel what we felt. We fear because the risk it takes to be vulnerable and loved means intentionally allowing someone the opportunity to hurt us, and we have already experienced enough hurt to last our lifetime.

LOVE FIGHTS FEAR

Ironically, the best way to defeat our fear of love is to choose to love. God's Word offers this encouragement in 1 John 4:18. "There is no fear in love. But perfect love drives out fear, because fear has to do with punishment. The one who fears in not made perfect in love."

Fear is self-centered: What will *they* do? Love is other-focused: What can *I* do? Fear is one of Satan's greatest weapons. He can't take away our salvation, but he sure tries to take away our effectiveness in living a life of purpose, influence, and love. If we dwell on our fears, we forfeit our ability to both give and receive the love we yearn to experience. When we choose to love, we are on the road to healing our wounded hearts.

The decision to love is a willingness to *engage*. The love that is most satisfying—that which is reciprocated—is also beyond our control. In order for someone to get to know us well enough to love us, we must be willing to contradict our coping mechanisms—we must be trusting, vulnerable, and willing to relinquish control.

We may be able to accept an intellectual belief that God empowers us to love. But love that is based in knowledge alone will only guilt-trip or shame us into acting right. However, we can ask God to help us connect the dots from our head to our heart.

LEARNING TO RECOGNIZE AND GIVE LOVE

Government officials charged with detecting counterfeit money study the real currency, not the imitation. As they become intimately knowledgeable regarding what makes a bill authentic, they are less likely to be fooled by one that is not genuine. When it comes to love, our life has been saturated with so many counterfeits that we can easily accept the imitation. God designs; Satan distorts. We misdefine the love God designed when we accept Satan's distortion.

We get involved in relationships with people who don't love us back, reinventing ourselves to win their love. Or we expect that anything less than continual bliss cannot be true love until we realize, as twenty-three-old Beth did, that "love is not all the awe-inspiring perfect emotion I once naively thought it was." Disillusioned, we may lower our expectations to such a degree that we hook up with the first person who wants us. And ultimately, we push away those who are capable of loving us well, because we don't even recognize real love when it comes along. It isn't what we know.

But our stories don't have to end there. As we allow ourselves to receive the love extended to us by our heavenly Father, we become confident that only in Him will we find our satisfaction and fulfillment. Indeed, by receiving God's love for us we can learn to recognize and give true love. In *A Love Worth Giving,* Max Lucado wrote:

> A marriage-saving love is not within us. A friendship-preserving devotion cannot be found in our hearts. We need help from an outside source. A transfusion. Would we love as God loves? Then we start by receiving God's love.
>
> We preachers have been guilty of skipping the first step. "Love each other!" we tell our churches. "Be patient, kind, forgiving," we urge. But instructing people to love without telling them they are

loved is like telling them to write a check without making a deposit. No wonder so many relationships are overdrawn. Hearts have insufficient love. The apostle John models the right sequence. He makes a deposit before he tells us to write the check. First, the deposit:

"God showed how much he loved us by sending his only Son into the world so that we might have eternal life through him. This is real love. It is not that we loved God, but that he loved us and sent his Son as a sacrifice to take away our sins" (1 John 4:9-10 NLT).

And then, having made such an outrageous, eye-opening deposit, John calls on you and me to pull out the checkbook, "Dear friends, since God loved us that much, we surely ought to love each other" (v. 11 NLT).

The secret to loving is living loved. This is the forgotten first step in relationships.[2]

If we long to love well, we must first receive God's love for us. We must let it nestle deep within our heart and fill the holes to overflowing. God knows us completely and loves us unconditionally. Out of His love for us, He offers to take away the hurts that hinder us, the scars that shame us, and the burdens that bury us.

Do you realize how much God loves you? You are His workmanship, "created in Christ Jesus to do good works, which God prepared in advance for us to do" (Ephesians 2:10). The Greek word for workmanship is *poieme* and refers to a masterpiece or work of art. We were fearfully and wonderfully made, no matter how we were conceived. Before we were even born, God delighted in our development. We aren't some junior-high art project that gets dumped in the trash. We are the Sistine Chapel, the Mona Lisa, the Last Supper. We were created to be oohed and aahed over, and God is our most frequent admirer. Our portraits hang in the

Louvre of heaven. His constant attention protects us from life's harshness and the danger of decay. It's almost unfathomable to imagine such extravagant love.

As we accept and receive God's lavish love, we cannot help but be transformed by it. Allow nothing in your attitudes and thinking to hinder the flow of this love. Ask God to give you a new heart—a heart capable of receiving His love—one that loves others out of the abundance of that love. This is a prayer that God promises to answer: "I will give you a new heart and put a new spirit in you; I will remove from you your heart of stone and give you a heart of flesh" (Ezekiel 36:26).

Putting Love into Action

We put love into action when we respond to others in ways that leave no doubt that the source of our love is God Himself.

We love our family when we choose to honor them. Megan shows love to her family with a tradition of sending each family member a birthday letter that tells both what she respects about them and what she has learned from them that year.

We love our friends as we choose to be accountable to them. Becca shows love to her roommate, Sarah, when she agrees to not watch television shows or movies that conflict with Sarah's more tender conscience.

We love those around us when we choose to see them as God sees them. Ryan shows love to Joe, the guy in his Bible study who always seems to be struggling with something, by initiating a get-together outside of small group.

And we love our spouse when we choose to regard our marriage as an indivisible illustration of God's love in the flesh, or as Mignon McLaughlin has said, "A successful marriage requires falling in love many times, always with the same person."[3]

In the days of my parents' separation, they read Anne Morrow Lindbergh's *Gift of the Sea*. I don't remember how I got the copy, which includes both my mom and dad's scribbled reflections, and though I never read it until I wrote this book, I clung to it as a memento of their marriage.

Anne speaks to the fluidity of romantic love this way,

> When you love someone you do not love them all the time, in exactly the same way, from moment to moment. It is an impossibility. It is even a lie to pretend to. And yet this is exactly what most of us demand. We have so little faith in the ebb and flow of life, of love, or relationships. We leap at the flow of the tide and resist in terror its ebb. We are afraid it will never return. We insist on permanency, on duration, on continuity; when the only continuity possible, in life as in love, is in growth, in fluidity—in freedom, in the sense that the dancers are free, barely touching as they pass, but partners in the same pattern.[4]

Love is a choice we are empowered to make. We know that our feelings of love are going to fade and flow back. We need to acknowledge that reality when our love is vibrant so that when it becomes dull, we dig in with a tenacious determination to honor our vow to love "for better *and for worse*" as we work to restore it back to better again.

And yet, we are still left with the million-dollar question: *How* do we love when the one we love is being selfish, hurtful, or just a flat-out jerk?

SEEING IMPERFECTIONS AS TOOLS FOR GROWTH

As we all know, a heart can experience deep hurt. But as believers we don't make it our goal to avoid hurt. Rather, our goal is to see others through God's eyes and love them as He loves us. In doing so, we offer others a tangible example of who God is and how He loves. As others hurt us, we consider the grace extended to us, and we learn to forgive by practicing forgiveness. If we have really given our heart to God, then we have forfeited our right to withhold love from others. Natural love responds to the attractive features in another person; it is a selfish impulse. Supernatural love is a conscious choice. As a feeling, love comes and goes without our control. When we view love as a choice, we are empowered to make love last.

Leslie Vernick, writing in *How to Act Right When Your Spouse Acts Wrong*, says, "Our choices reveal what we love the most, what we fear, what is of ultimate value to us, and what we think we need in life—in other words, our choices expose the dominant desires of our heart."[5]

What is your dominant desire? How does it play out in your interactions with others and your decision to choose to love? As we bask in the unconditional love of a Father who will never leave us even when we disappoint Him, we are willing to accept the imperfections of others.

One of the thirty-years-married couples I interviewed was stopped short when I posed this question, "How do you show love to your spouse when you don't feel love toward him or her?" After several moments, the husband replied, "I don't think I can answer that question because I don't know that it's possible *not* to love my wife. Of course, we have our bad days and our inopportune moments, but our shared existence is so entwined that the love I have for her—quirks and all—is inseparable from my love for myself. The question is not, Do I feel love? But, How deeply do I feel love?" For this couple, years of choosing to love has made loving choices automatic.

As we become people who are able to receive love—from God and others—we begin to see others not as those who could potentially hurt us, but as people loved by God, brought into our life for a purpose. As we become aware of the imperfections of others—and they, of ours—we can be tools for each other's growth.

Susan and Bob were married less than ten years when she first suspected his infidelity. They had married right out of high school, and at twenty-eight, Susan was the overwhelmed mother of three. She kept her fears to herself, ignoring peoples' stares and whispers when she picked up the kids at school and ran her household errands. A woman of prayer, Susan pleaded with God to return her husband's heart to her. Things finally came to a head when Susan returned early from a meeting at church to find her husband in their bed with another woman. In the confrontation that followed, Bob informed Susan matter-of-factly that he no longer loved her and was moving out.

Though many of Susan's friends counseled her to seek a divorce, she was more concerned with demonstrating to her children the limitless forgiveness of God. She refused to speak poorly of their father, though at times that meant she rarely said much about him at all. Several months after George moved out, Susan had to sell the home she loved and move in with her parents, along with her three children. George did not leave the area and continued to engage in casual affairs, much to the embarrassment of Susan and her children. Susan asked her friend Mary to pray with her for her shattered marriage and to hold her accountable to be open to reconciliation, should George ever return.

Susan had to continuously fight off resentment, especially when news of George's latest fling came her way, when she became frustrated with her dependence on her parents, or when she felt she deserved more than life was giving her. Despite the encouragement of well-meaning friends that she give up on George, Susan poured herself into serving at her church, spending time with her children, and interceding each day for her husband.

Her middle child, Charles, told me,

Everyone thought Mom was in denial. Most of her friends told her to get a divorce and move on with her life, because God wanted her to be happy and we needed a father figure. We kids wondered what made our dad worth fighting for. But seven long years later, God answered my mom's prayers: Dad came home. A friend's child was killed in a car wreck and that loss made Dad realize what he lost when he walked away from us. He didn't know if Mom would take him back, but he had heard that she would consider it. When he came home, he was humble, broken, and willing to do whatever was necessary to rebuild my mom's trust.

So they started dating—one night each week on the town and another in counseling. Dad started coming to church with us again. And then, fourteen months later, on their anniversary, Mom and Dad had a rededication ceremony in front of all the people who never thought the day would come. And that night, I finally understood what God's love looks like because I saw it demonstrated in my mom all those years. She never condoned what Dad did, but she didn't condemn him either. Their anniversary marks the day I became a Christian. And now that I'm married, her model means so much more to me. I'm a pastor today because I learned from my mom that no one is beyond God's grace.

Susan made the choice to love, and in so doing helped others understand God's love for us.

WE HAVE A CHOICE

As we begin to let God's unbelievable love into our heart, our mind, and our soul, we can't help but share the sheer joy of it with others around us, regardless of their reaction to us. As we learn to be satisfied with the love that God has for us, we stop putting expectations on others that they were not created to fill. We release ourselves from the futility of letting others dictate our happiness because our joy now depends on Someone who is utterly stable and secure. We no longer ask God to make us happy, and instead ask how to bring a smile to His face as we bring joy to those around us.

As children of divorce, we crave security. We crave control to regain the stability we lost as a result of divorce. Yet, we have within our power the possibility to either establish new patterns or repeat the patterns of our past. We can choose to heal; we can choose to love.

Word

> Be imitators of God, therefore, as dearly loved children and live a
> life of love, just as Christ loved us. (Ephesians 5:1-2)

Reflect

- What are some of the fears you face, especially in light of your desire to love? Contrast your fears with truth and reasons why you can face those fears successfully.
- If fearing to love and choosing to love are opposite ends of a continuum, where do you see yourself on that continuum?
- How has fear influenced your decision to love?
- What shadow beliefs have you accepted about love? Contrast them with the truth.
- Based on your interactions with others, what do you think they would say is your dominant desire? Would you agree or disagree?

Challenge

Look up *love* in a concordance or online through a search engine like www.bible.gospelcom.net. Read through the verses and list the attributes of love. Next to each one, write a practical way to demonstrate that attribute to someone you love.

Read

Bold Love by Dan B. Allender and Tremper Longman III (Nav-Press, 1993)

Hiding from Love by Henry Cloud and John Townsend (Zondervan, 1996)

Love Is a Decision by Gary Smalley and John Trent (Word, 1992)

A Love Worth Giving by Max Lucado (W Publishing, 2002)

The Secret of Loving by Josh McDowell (Tyndale, 1987)

Unbreakable Bonds: Practicing the Art of Loving and Being Loved by Cheryl Meier and Paul Meier (Baker, 2002)

Embrace Our Identity As Abba's Child

For much of my twenties, I immersed myself in my work as a way to satisfy my yearning for both an identity and a sense of belonging. Even though I would have told you that my identity was in Christ, a brief look at my time commitments and goals would have indicated otherwise. My career catered to my coping mechanism: Attain perfection with proven results. I could, for the most part, control my career choices. In my work I had a place of belonging—at my own desk and with my own family of fellow employees. I had a role—a title with outlined responsibilities. And because I worked in a Christian environment, I could rationalize that my eternally minded service Monday through Friday was enough to please God and satisfy me.

When I was twenty-nine, I began taking stock of my life. It didn't start intentionally: One morning I woke up and wondered if I would ever marry. I wondered if I had focused so much on my career that I had denied myself the opportunity to create what I *really* wanted: a family of my own. I had just closed on a condo and adopted a puppy, two very significant steps toward my goal of settling down and finding home.

Shortly after my morning musing, I was in Nashville on business. Each year, Gospel Music Week begins with an all-industry worship service. Several artists made up the informal choir that night and the rest of us praised God from our seats in the historic Ryman. We had just finished a song about God as our Father when I noticed Billy Buchanan from the band Fusebox. As others around him were kneeling or praying with their heads down, Billy stood tall with his arms outstretched upward, as a child trusting his father to pick him up. I immediately saw a picture of how God longed to love and hold me. However, in my own independent pursuits, I had allowed Him access only according to my own agenda. I realized that I lacked that reckless trust of a child. I mourned that I could not remember a time when I ran like that into my daddy's (or stepdaddy's) arms. I dropped to my knees and asked God's forgiveness for holding Him out at the same respectful distance that I held out my parents. I asked him to show me evidence of His fatherly love.

At that moment, my name tag dropped to the floor. As I picked it up, I saw my name in a new light. Long before I was born, God knew my name—Jen Abbas. Do you know that my name literally means "Daddy's Jen"? Abba is the most intimate and affectionate name for God, and that is the name He chose for me. When I struggle, wondering if I'm a priority to anyone, the Creator of the universe reminds me each time I write my name that before there was time, He *chose* to love me and He will never cease loving me! Can we even comprehend that kind of love?

Many pastors and writers have compared the love of God to the love they have for their children. The analogy is a fitting one, but not one I can really relate to as a single person. Yet, every morning, my Shih Tzu, Bailey, starts to wake up before me. As consciousness begins to rouse her, her eyes fix on me. She knows she can't go where she wants to go (outside!) until I open the door for her. Because she is focused on me, she can respond to my most subtle movement. It strikes me how infrequently I wake with my thoughts so focused on God that I am intimately attuned to His will.

When I return home, Bailey is ecstatically joyful to see me and lets me know in no uncertain terms just how pleased she is. She jumps up, wanting to be held. She darts between my legs as I walk to drop my things in the kitchen. As I get a snack, she sits in rapt attention. Nothing could be more satisfying to her than to simply be in my presence. How I long to have that same enthusiasm for my Savior.

When night falls and I am settled in my office to write, Bailey comes to me and tells me, with pleading eyes or a gentle touch of her paw, that she wants to be near me. She is not afraid of rejection. She knows I love her, even when I don't respond to her requests immediately. How I marvel at the privilege to approach my Abba Daddy with that same confidence.

John 1:12 states, "Yet to all who received him, to those who believed in his name, he gave the right to become children of God." If ever we doubt the depth of God's longing for us, we need only to consider that the blood His Son shed is the crimson love that made our adoption possible. God in three persons provides the supportive family we idealize. God, our Father and Creator, walks before us. All that we will experience is already known to Him. Jesus, our Savior and Friend, walks beside us. He is our constant companion. The Holy Spirit, our Comforter and Encourager, walks behind us. He intercedes on our behalf. All around us are our siblings, our brothers and sisters in the family of God, sharing in both our sorrows and successes. We are not victims of our pasts; we are now sons and daughters of a Father who loves us more than we can ever imagine.

Kevin Max, in his book *Unfinished Work* wrote, "God doesn't know us by our labels. He knows each of us by name."[1] Not only does God know our names, but He also understands that we are unfinished works from a spiritual perspective of imperfection and in terms of our healing. Just as our spiritual objective is to grow *toward* a more divine default, our goal as adult children of divorce is not complete closure, but *continual* closure. As we develop an ongoing awareness of our shadow beliefs, we can shine upon them the light of truth. As we anticipate our triggers, we can address each of them in a way that neutralizes their power to defeat us. We'll have good days and we'll have bad days, but each day we can hold on to the hope God offers us.

This book requires a lot of hard emotional work. Don't assume that just because you're reading the final pages you have come to the end of the lesson. This book is meant only to be a catalyst to get you going. Only you will be able to determine what you must do on your journey.

We face a limitation as children of divorce because, at this time, we don't have widely accepted societal permission to talk about our lingering hurts. But just because our pain is not understood does not mean we should suffer in silence. Perhaps you and I can create that cultural awareness as we admit that a generation is being blindsided by unspoken sorrows, shadow beliefs, and trigger events. We must give ourselves permission to acknowledge and grieve the scars we still bear decades after the divorce decision. I'm optimistic that just as our society has become aware of the needs of other unique groups, society's eyes will soon be opened to our needs and our hurts, if by nothing else but the sheer number of our names.

As you read these final words, I hope your heart is a little lighter and your perspective more positive. It's been a hard road for us to walk, but I want you to know that even when the route seems overwhelming, you are never alone. God, our Father, walks with us, *through* the valleys and *to* the high points. In the two years since WaterBrook asked me to write this book, I have had a team of people praying over every step of the process. They have also been praying for you! This dedicated core has joined with me in praying for you—that you would be drawn to read this book; that you would make peace—with God and your family; that you would grow in vibrant faith; that you would skillfully redefine your family in a way that nurtures your needs; that you would find home for yourself with a family of friends; that you would seek wholeness and find it; that you would learn to trust and develop an inner circle of Accountable Advisors who will share life with you at the deepest, most intimate level; that you would learn to anticipate your triggers and choose to respond to them in a way that enhances the future you desire; that you would create a new model of marriage that is characterized by lifelong joy and fulfillment; that you would choose to love and receive the love of others; and most of all, we have prayed that you will embrace your identity as Abba's much loved child.

> How great is the love the Father has lavished on us, that we should be called children of God! (1 John 3:1)

An Invitation to Become Abba's Child

R egardless of our relationship with our earthly father, we are invited to have a relationship with a Father God who promises never to leave us or forsake us. This invitation is presented in the person of Jesus Christ, a human picture of grace.

So what is grace? It's as simple as this: God knows we cannot live perfect lives, so He provided the way for us to deal perfectly with our imperfections.

Since God created us, we ultimately belong to Him, much in the same way that our children are a part of us. Rather than making us to be a bunch of robots, God gave us the ability to make our own choices. Like the educationally minded parent who offers choices and consequences for different behaviors, God set a standard of expectation (perfection) and a clearly laid out consequence for failing to achieve that objective (permanent separation from Him). Ever since Adam and Eve in the garden, we humans have shown a fondness for doing our own thing. While we may not feel the effects of our choices down here, we will be held accountable for our actions when we die.

From a worldly perspective, we might feel a bit like the teen convinced that a nonnegotiable midnight curfew is unfair. From an eternal perspective, God is perfect and can only share eternity with those who choose to share that holiness.

Since we know we are neither perfect nor holy, it seems we'd be in a bind. And yet, God planned to deal with our imperfection in an incredible way. How many of us would create a plan so bizarre as to require our child to die in order that someone else could have the opportunity to become a part of our family? How many of us would allow our innocent son to be held responsible for the crime of another? On that cross with the Savior so central to Christianity hung all the sins we would ever commit. Jesus bore the consequences for all our wrongs as if He had committed them Himself. Think about that. When Jesus died over two thousand years ago, all of the sins we have ever committed and ever will commit were future sins. When Jesus died, so did the power of those sins to separate us from the God who loves us. The rightful consequence of every white lie, every lustful thought, every vengeful act was paid in full on that bloody day.

The story does not end with death, however, because the God who created the universe has power over even the rules that order that universe. After three days, Jesus came back to life, the consequences for our sin completely paid. For those who acknowledge this sacrifice personally, Christ provides the lens through which His Father sees us as having the same level of perfection that only rightfully belongs to Him.

We might be willing to do something nice for someone we love, or even someone we like. Sometimes we might do something because our favor persuades the other to extend a courtesy to us. But how many of us would sacrifice personally if we knew our offering would be unnoticed or unused or unaccepted? Jesus died a horrible, humiliating death on a cross with the full knowledge that millions would never even acknowledge His sacrifice. He died simply to give us that choice.

Our heavenly Father calls you by name, to offer you a permanent place in His home, access to His vast resources and an unconditional love that will never let you go. If you would like to begin a new life in Christ, please consider making this prayer your own:

Abba Daddy,

I have had much hurt in my life. Those who should have protected me didn't always provide the shield I needed. I have been let down. I have been made to feel that I was not a priority. I have felt unloved.

And now I realize that I have hurt You by choosing to do things that displease You and failing to meet the standard You had every right as my spiritual Father to set for me. I'm sorry, God, and I ask for Your forgiveness.

You, too, know what it's like to have family taken from You. You sent Your Son to die so that I could be a part of Your family. Thank You. I want to live my life in a way that pleases You. I am so thankful that You don't require me to make these changes on my own or as a prerequisite for Your love. Thank You for giving me a permanent place in Your family; I need to know I have a place to belong. Thank You for Your unconditional love; I need to know I've never strayed too far. Thank You for sharing Your resources; I need to know that someone will provide for me. Thank You for Your faithfulness; I need to know I am worthy of commitment. Thank You for this new life, because I need to know there is a purpose for my pain.

Amen

If you are experiencing God's perfect and secure love for the first time or want to know more about spiritual adoption by our heavenly Abba, I would love to hear from you. Please e-mail me at jen@jenabbas.com.

A Retreat of Silence

WHAT IS A RETREAT OF SILENCE?

A retreat of silence is an extended period, usually several hours, in which a person seeks seclusion from outside distractions for the sole purpose of spending time with God, reflecting on his or her life, and discerning God's will.

WHAT SHOULD I BRING?

Bring a Bible, notebook, and pen or pencil. That's it, nothing else. This is not the time to listen to music, have a deep conversation with a friend, or enjoy a snack.

WHAT SHOULD I DO?

Just as it takes extended periods of time to build a relationship with a friend or significant other, it takes time to build a relationship with God. This retreat of silence is a good opportunity to purposefully listen to what God has to say about your relationship with Him.

HOW DO I GET STARTED?

1. *Pray.* Dedicate this time for God's purposes. Ask God what He desires for your life. Ask Him to quiet your mind so that you can really listen without distraction.

2. *Show your appreciation.* Write down or say thank You for all of the things God has done for you.

3. *Reflect.* Consider each area of your life in terms of its testimony to God's influence on it.

Spiritual
- Do I talk with God daily?
- How often am I reading His word, and is it making an impact on my lifestyle?
- Is there someone to whom I have given complete freedom to hold me accountable to the things I say I do?
- How has God gifted me, and how am I using those gifts to serve others?
- What is the next step God has for me so I can better reflect His character in this area?

Personal
- Is there anything about my interactions with the opposite sex that is not pleasing to God?
- When I have a free moment, what do I tend to think about? Does this thought encourage or discourage intimacy with God?
- If God were to call me to a new job, new city, new relationship, and so on, would I be willing to obey?
- Is there anything that I know God has called me to do, but I'm hesitating to do? What is holding me back?
- What is the next step God has for me so I can better reflect His character in this area?

Financial
- Is there anything about my finances that is not pleasing to God?

- If an accountant were to look at my expenses, what would he or she say is the most important thing to me?
- What would I be willing to give up so that someone else could have their needs met?
- What is my responsibility to God concerning the finances entrusted to me?
- What is the next step God has for me so I can better reflect His character in this area?

Professional
- Is there anything about my professional life that is not pleasing to God?
- If a coworker were to look at my work habits, what would that person say is the most important thing to me?
- Is the job that I have the one that God desires me to be in at this time? If so, what does He wish me to accomplish for His purpose? If not, what is keeping me from moving on?
- What drives me to do my work?
- What is the next step God has for me so I can better reflect His character in this area?

Physical
- Is there anything about my actions or attitudes about my appearance that is not pleasing to God?
- Based on my thoughts and actions, is this area of my life more or less important to me than my spiritual life?
- Am I doing anything intentionally with my appearance, dress, or interactions that would cause a brother or sister to stumble?
- Am I doing anything intentionally with my thoughts or motivations that I would not want to admit to someone else?

- What is the next step God has for me so I can better reflect His character in this area?

4. *Be silent and listen.* Take at least twenty minutes to simply be still. Write down any insights, scriptures, or plans of action that come to mind.

5. *Read.* Be ready to look in Scripture for passages that apply to what God is showing you, and write down your insights. This might be a good time to work on memorizing a few key verses.

6. *Commit to action.*
   - What does God desire to teach me? How will I learn it?
   - How does God desire to work in or through me? How will I do it?
   - What has God convicted me to give up or start doing? To whom will I be accountable to follow through with it?

A Marriage Retreat

WHAT IS A MARRIAGE RETREAT?

A marriage retreat is an extended period in which a couple seeks seclusion from outside distractions for the sole purpose of spending time with God and each other to renew their commitments to each other and to God.

WHAT SHOULD WE BRING?

In addition to items you would normally pack for a weekend getaway, add the following:

- Bible, notebook, pens, highlighters
- Bible study of interest to both of you (on any topic)
- books for the two of you to read together
- copy of your budget
- copy of your marriage contract or family constitution, if applicable
- video of your wedding (if you'll have a means to watch it), and/or a copy of your wedding vows
- copy of your goals from your previous retreat, if applicable
- willingness to examine and discuss the state of your marriage and faith honestly
- desire to improve the two most important relationships in your life
- a plan for the weekend (You don't need a fifteen-minute increment itinerary of the entire weekend, but it should be planned enough that it differs from a typical vacation or getaway)

What Should We Do?

With all the demands on a couple's life, it's a challenge to carve out time simply to enjoy each other's company and review the goals and dreams for your marriage. Just as you regularly take your vehicle to the shop for a tune-up, getting away for a weekend to focus on your spouse and your relationships with God is an intentional way of checking the health of your marriage and spiritual lives. Each couple should determine goals for their retreat. A sample itinerary follows:

Recognize
- Recognize the presence of God in your marriage and in your life. Pray that He will guide you and give you discernment to see your marriage as it is. Pray that His presence will be felt, His influence will be compelling, and His plans will be clear.
- Agree that God's Word takes precedence over either spouse's opinion. Be ready to search the Scriptures together without pre-conceived notions or motivation to prove the other wrong.
- While some words may be expressed this weekend that hurt to hear, commit to share them in love and receive them knowing that they are spoken for the betterment of your marriage. A good test to tell if you are speaking in love is to consider how you would inter-pret those same words spoken in the same tone by your spouse. Consider the validity of your spouse's words before responding to them. The overriding goal is to build up the "we" of your marriage. Attacking each other is counterproductive to this goal.

Remember
- Tell each other again the story of your courtship with God. What made you decide to believe in Jesus Christ as your Savior? How has that decision changed your life?

- Retell the story of your courtship with each other. Remind yourselves why you fell in love. Remember the hopes and dreams you had as you started your life together. You may want to write them down for the next step.

Reflect

- Looking at your list of mutual goals and plans, consider how well you have met your expectations. Would you like to change or add any goals?
- If this is not your first retreat, review your five goals from the last retreat. Talk about your progress toward achieving them.
- Think about your marriage relationship. What do you like best about being married? When you brag about your spouse to others (and you should!), what do you say?
- What has been the most difficult adjustment in your marriage this year? How has the relationship compared to your expectations?
- What is the health of your "we"? Are the wishes or goals of either of you more dominant? If so, what will you do to elevate the "we"?
- Are you willing to make a change in your behavior (provided it does not compromise your convictions) if it would improve your spouse's view of the marriage? If both agree to do so, write down the item that you would like to see your spouse change, and then exchange lists. Discuss them until you understand why this issue is important to the other, and decide together whether or not you will implement the change.
- Think about your faith. Share how it has matured in the last year. What issues is God addressing in you now? Is there anything you need to confess to each other?
- Discuss the role of faith in your marriage. Is God a central member, or is He more like an out-of-state in-law? What action can

you take to make Him more involved in your relationship as a
couple?
- Take a few hours individually for a retreat of silence. Set a time
and place to reconvene.

Retreat

- Individually, complete the retreat of silence exercise.

Reconvene

- Share your retreat of silence experiences. In what way did you
have similar convictions for change? Were there any areas of
opposite convictions?
- If you had differences, discuss how you will resolve that issue.
- Pray together and commit to hold each other accountable to
your convictions.

Readjust

- Consider what the upcoming year will bring and create a plan
of action to do those things well.
- Evaluate the effectiveness of your budget and make any necessary
changes, incorporating the needs of a growing family and/or
planned purchases.
- If you have a marriage contract or family constitution, examine
it carefully and make any necessary adjustments.

Renew

- Read your wedding vows to each other. How well have you
upheld your promises? How has time changed your understanding of that covenant?
- If you weren't Christians when you married, how have your relationships with Christ changed your understanding of marriage?

• Regardless of your spiritual history, take some time together to
  come up with a new set of vows more specific to the current state
  of your marriage (for example, conflict resolution, parenthood,
  and so on). Here is an illustration:

I join with you this day in a covenant not between you and me
but between the two of us and God. I promise to choose to love
you for the rest of my days as I strive not only to make you
happy but to make us holy. I promise that together we will
embrace both the joys and hardships that God will allow us to
face. I commit to creating a marriage in which our children, our
family, our friends, and others will see Christ in us and through
us as we model His love, His life, and His reconciliation. I
promise to be faithful to you in heart, mind, body, and spirit,
from better to worse to better again, till death brings us new life.

• Create another vow to be spoken to God, inviting Him to be a
  valued third member of your marriage. Pray that vow to Him
  together. For example:

Abba Father,

We come to you together, recognizing the oneness that You
established in us that day when we first spoke our vows of marriage. We acknowledge that You are the creator of marriage and
that in it we are a human example of Your love for all people.
We invite You to be the center of our life and leader of this marriage. We thank You for Your unfailing faithfulness, servant-
hearted humility, reconciling grace, and unconditional love. We
pray that others will see those qualities in us, as we strive to make
You the prominent member of this relationship. Help us always

to submit to Your leadership and standard. We thank You for
Your promise to bind us together till death brings us new life.

Read

- One of the advantages of reading together is that books provide
an objective platform for discussing the issues of life. Take some
time to read to each other, pausing often to discuss your thoughts
on the topic.

Review

- Look over your notes from the weekend's discussion. What was
your favorite part? What was the hardest? What was the most
surprising?
- Of all the things you revealed, discovered, and discussed, choose
five items that you will focus on as a couple. When you get
home, keep the list posted in a place where the two of you will
see it each day.

Recommit

- Reassure each other of your mutual love (be specific) and commit
to the permanence of your relationship.
- Thank God for this time together and for the gift of your spouse.
- Pray together for God's help as you incorporate changes or make
adjustments to your marriage.

Relax

- Take time to enjoy each other's company. Pretend you're on your
honeymoon again, viewing your spouse with that same wide-eyed
wonder and appreciation.

A Letter to Divorced Parents

Dear Parent,

Thank you for picking up this book! I realize you may not like what I have to say, because it contradicts what we would *all* like to believe—that divorce is a temporary crisis. I hope, though, that you will hear me out. The fact that you picked up this book tells me that your compassion and love for your child is strong, and I'm so glad you are willing to listen to what your child may not be able to articulate to you. I know you did the very best you could at the time you made that painful decision to divorce.

I pray that you will read this book with an open heart. Please understand that this is not a book about blame. It's not a parent-bashing book, but it does acknowledge, affirm, and address the unique issues your child has to face as a result of your divorce. While you may have been able to put to death your divorce, for your child it is the funeral that never ends, because we want and need both parents to be a part of our lives, for all of our lives.

I hope that you will take the following suggestions to heart as you continue on your own path of healing:

1. *Don't put us in the middle.* We are not your messengers. We are your children. Please don't make us choose sides. It's just not fair. Part of growing up is learning that our parents aren't perfect. We learned that lesson sooner than we should have. We want to love you both; please don't make it hard for us to do so.

2. *Be available.* You may be ready to talk about the divorce. We may not be there yet, at least not with you. In the meantime, let us know that we are free to ask any question without getting a bitter or defensive response. As we heal, we may feel a need to fill in the holes in our history. The divorce is part of our lives. If we can talk about it (not fight about it or justify it), we can learn from it.

3. *Reflect.* Think about why your marriage failed and be ready to tell us what you have learned. We want desperately to know we aren't destined to divorce. Consider what you would do differently and why. Be ready to share with us your wisdom if we ask.

4. *Write us a letter.* Tell us why you are proud of us. Be specific. Make a list of the good things that came from the marriage (including us!). Write down the reasons why you first fell in love with our other parent. If we have those positive characteristics, tell us. We need to hear this from you.

5. *Adjust for our convenience.* As adults, it's really hard for us to balance the time we spend with both sets of parents, especially around holidays and special events, and even more so if we feel we're in a no-win situation. We're not asking you to be friends. We're simply asking that you don't make things harder than they need to be.

6. *Be prepared for a wide range of emotions.* We may have blocked out a lot of memories as a way of coping. As adults, those memories may come back without warning, and we may respond to them with anger, confusion, or any other emotion. Sometimes, in frustration, the emotion may seem directed at you. Realize that our response is a delayed reaction to something that you may have already processed. Let us express it so we can deal with it.

7. *Don't talk negatively about our other parent.* We have a right to love you both. Talk to a friend or counselor or pastor about the things that drive you crazy about our other parent. Don't tell us. We need to know the good stuff.

8. *Ask for our forgiveness.* As you focused on your adjustment, you may not have spent as much time with us as you should have, and our lives are harder because of it. Only a perfect person could deal with all those emotions without causing hurt to us. Your willingness to acknowledge that hurt will go a long way in our healing, as well as your own.

9. *Legitimize our loss.* Please don't force us to feel okay with everything that happened. We probably don't. Most likely, we will always feel this loss because it is just as significant as losing a limb or sense. It doesn't mean we can't be healthy, but life will always be just a little different for us.

10. *Tell us you love us.* We can never, *ever* hear it enough. Sometimes it feels like the divorce of your ex was really a divorce of us. We saw from your example that love may be conditional, earned, and fleeting. Prove us wrong.

—Jen Abbas

Notes

Chapter 1

1. Both statistics are from the National Center for Health Statistics, Monthly Vital Statistics reports, as reported by Patrick F. Fagan and Robert Rector in their online report "The Effect of Divorce on America," 5 June 2000 (http://www.heritage.org/library/backgrounder/bg1373.html).

2. Maggie Gallagher, *The Abolition of Marriage: How We Destroy Lasting Love* (Washington, D.C.: Regnery Publishing, 1996), 76.

3. PBS interview with Judith Wallerstein, January 2000. http://www.pbs.org/newshour/forum/january01/wallerstein.html.

4. Barbara Dafoe Whitehead, *The Divorce Culture* (New York: Knopf, 1997), 47-65.

5. DivorceMagazine.net's "Statistics on Divorce," (Sources: U.S. Census Bureau, National Center for Health Statistics, Americans for Divorce Reform, Institute for Equality in Marriage, American Association for Single People, Ameristat, Public Agenda).

6. Judith Wallerstein and Sandra Blakeslee, *Second Chances: Men, Women and Children a Decade After Divorce* (New York: Houghton Mifflin, 1996), 56-64.

7. E. Mavis Hetherington and John Kelly, *For Better or for Worse: Divorce Reconsidered* (New York: Norton, 2002), as cited in "Impact of Divorce Debatable" by Kathy Boccella, 4 February 2002, at http://www.gazette.com/stories/0204/life2.php?section=3.

8. Elizabeth Marquardt, "We're Successful, and Hurt," *Washington Post,* 2 February 2002, B5.

9. Wallerstein and Blakeslee, *Second Chances,* 7.

10. Wallerstein and Blakeslee, *Second Chances,* paraphrased, 11.

11. Wallerstein and Blakeslee, *Second Chances,* paraphrased, 14.

12. Steve Beard, "Childhood Divorce Fuels Fire of New Rock," *Washington Times,* 4 October 2002. You can also find a list of lyrics on my Web site: http://www.abbaschild.org.

13. Stephanie Staal, *The Love They Lost: Living with the Legacy of Our Parents' Divorce* (New York: Delacorte, 2000), 2.

14. Staal, *Love They Lost,* 246.

Chapter 2

1. Josh McDowell, *The Secret of Loving* (Wheaton: Tyndale, 1985), 102-3.

2. My Web site includes the lyrics to several songs written from the perspective of children of divorce.

3. Stephanie Staal, *The Love They Lost: Living with the Legacy of Our Parents' Divorce* (New York: Delacorte, 2000), 23.

4. Brennan Manning, *The Ragamuffin Gospel* (Sisters, Oreg.: Multnomah, 1990), 61.

5. Interview with Gary Chapman for FamilyChristian.com, 20 February 2002.

Chapter 3

1. Mike Nappa, *Growing Up Fatherless* (Grand Rapids: Revell, 2003), 15-6.

2. See Luke 15:11-32.

3. Elizabeth Marquardt, "Children of Divorce: Stories of Exile," www.americanvalues.org/html/3_stories_of_exile, February 2001.

4. The author of this Internet inspiration is unknown.

5. Ephesians 6:17.

6. The author of this popular Internet inspiration is unknown.

Chapter 4

1. Found at the CommunityZero.com/AKOD message board.

2. Dr. Henry Cloud and Dr. John Townsend, *Boundaries* (Grand Rapids: Zondervan, 1992), front flap.0

3. Found at http://www.christianitytoday.com/cpt/2001/004/17.48.html.

Chapter 5

1. *Real World Casting Special,* MTV, Spring 2001.

2. Found at http://www.americanvalues.org/html/3_ministering_to_cod.

3. My thanks to Sue, who detailed this service on her Web site: http://www .angelfire.com/sc/GoddessSue/funeral.html.

4. Interview with Steven Curtis Chapman, July 2001. Found at www .familychristian.com/music/interviews/stevencchapman.

Chapter 6

1. Stormie Omartian, *Lord, I Want to Be Whole* (Nashville: Nelson, 2000), 3.

2. Drs. Les and Leslie Parrott, *Relationships* (Grand Rapids: Zondervan, 1998), 20.

Chapter 7

1. Found at http://dictionary.reference.com/search?q=trust.

2. John Gray, Ph.D., *Men Are from Mars, Women Are from Venus* (New York: HarperCollins, 1992), 30-3.

Chapter 8

1. Judith Wallerstein and Sandra Blakeslee, *Second Chances: Men, Women and Children a Decade After Divorce* (Boston: Houghton Mifflin, 1989), 59.

2. Wallerstein and Blakeslee, *Second Chances,* 60, 63.

3. Beverly Rodgers and Tom Rodgers, *Adult Children of Divorced Parents: Making Your Marriage Work* (San Jose: Resource Publications, 2002), 43-4.

4. Grant Norsworthy of the Paul Colman Trio offered this advice to me after an interview.

Chapter 9

1. Interview with Bebo Norman, 15 July 2002, in Los Angeles.
2. Linda Waite and Maggie Gallagher, *The Case for Marriage* (New York: Doubleday, 2000), 148.
3. Gary Thomas, *Sacred Marriage* (Grand Rapids: Zondervan, 2000), 32.
4. Thomas, *Sacred Marriage,* 34-5.
5. Dr. Fred Lowery, *Covenant Marriage* (West Monroe, La.: Howard, 2002), 24.
6. Stephen Arterburn and Fred Stoeker, *Every Woman's Desire* (Colorado Springs: WaterBrook, 2001), 54.
7. Dr. Henry Cloud and Dr. John Townsend, *God Will Make a Way* (Nashville: Integrity, 2002), 121-2.
8. Adapted from the article, "The Resolutions for Building a Strong Family," found at http://www.flc.org/hfl/flm04.htm.
9. The actual quote used *charity* rather than *love,* but given the change in meaning, the latter word better reflects Augustine's intention.

Chapter 10

1. Larry Crabb, *Inside Out* (Colorado Springs: NavPress, 1998), 98-9.
2. Max Lucado, *A Love Worth Giving* (Nashville: W Publishing, 2002), 7-8.
3. Found at http://www.quotegarden.com.
4. Anne Morrow Lindbergh, *Selections from Gift from the Sea: Hallmark Edition* (New York: Random House, 1955), 47.
5. Leslie Vernick, *How to Act Right When Your Spouse Acts Wrong* (Colorado Springs: WaterBrook, 2001), 112-3.

Conclusion

1. Kevin Max, *Unfinished Work* (Nashville: Nelson, 2001), 169.

About the Author

Jen Abbas is an adult child of divorce who faced parental divorces at ages six and eighteen. At age twenty-two, Jen was given the journal her parents kept from the beginning of their courtship until the day their divorce was final. This family memoir started Jen on a journey to discover how children of divorce can break free from the negative patterns created by their past. Jen makes her home in Grand Rapids, Michigan.

Jen Abbas's home on the Web for adult children of divorce is www.JenAbbas.com. The site provides articles, resources, news, interviews, booking information, and a link to her blog, www.GenerationExFiles.blogspot.com.

Jen would love to hear your story and answer your personal questions. You may e-mail her at jen@jenabbas.com.

FAMILYLIFE
Publishing™

www.familylife.com